The Making
of a Quaker College

Reminiscence from a Significant
Contributor to George Fox College

by Milo C. Ross

BARCLAY PRESS
Newberg, Oregon

The Making of a Quaker College

Published by Barclay Press, Newberg, Oregon
www.barclaypress.com
www.barclaypress.com/Ross

© 2015 by Barclay Press

Printed in the United States of America

ISBN 978-1-59498-035-0

COVER CREDITS: Photo of Milo and Alice Ross and the graphic
presentation of the Shambaugh Library mural are courtesy of the
George Fox University Archives. The mural "The Muse — A Search
for Knowledge," was created by Byron Gardner.

contents

Foreword

BY ARTHUR O. ROBERTS

M ILO ROSS and I interacted in two distinct time periods: the
first when he served as pastor of the Greenleaf (Idaho) Friends
Church during my teen years, the second when as colleagues we
ministered at George Fox College—he as president and I as professor. In both venues Milo excelled as a visionary, a nurturer, and an
enabler. Strong Christian faith sustained his ministry. He possessed
a creative mind, and had a passion to serve. I offer a few reflections
about each era.

When in 1936 Milo and Helen Ross came to minister at
Greenleaf Friends Church children and youth responded warmly to
them. During my high school years Milo gave our youth fellowship
a boost by taking us on moonlight desert outings. He helped boys
and girls treat each other with respect; he nurtured our Christian
faith through Spirit-guided sermons and conversations. With area
pastors he organized visits to other areas of the yearly meeting. A
memorable trek by truck to Twin Rocks camp on the Oregon coast
helped us Idaho kids form friendships with other Quaker youth—
overcoming provincialism. He adapted to new technology by providing a radio ministry, the *Quaker Hour*.

Other persons who were children or youth under Milo's ministry—especially at the Medford (Oregon) Friends Church, which
Milo pastored following his stint at Greenleaf—could relate similar stories. For example, Ruth Alice (Heather) Gardner cherishes a

Bible Milo gave to her for inviting the most people to special evangelistic services he was conducting at Springbrook Friends Church in Newberg, Oregon.

Milo helped me regain faith in God after my father died from pneumonia. I had prayed Papa would recover. He didn't. On the day Papa died I beat my head against a locust tree in our back yard and asked God why. Milo Ross served as God's minister to restore my faith. For the next father-son banquet he quietly arranged for a church member — a local miller — to take me as his boy for the evening. I still recall riding in his big Packard car.

Milo became my mentor — a sort of Paul to Timothy relationship. He nudged elders to discern the call of God to their youth. He facilitated gospel team ministry, with an elder hauling us kids to isolated communities to sing, read Scripture, and, yes, to "preach." I cherish what Quakers dub a "minute of service" signed by J. Allen Dunbar, clerk of the meeting, liberating me for ministry. It reads: "Though not a minister, Arthur is a capable Christian worker." I was only seventeen years old! Four years later, upon graduation from George Fox College (which Milo counseled me to attend) the Greenleaf church supported my recording as a Friends minister. The yearly meeting concurred. Lives of other future leaders such as Mahlon and Hazel Macy and Jack and Geraldine Willcuts were impacted similarly.

When Milo Ross became president of the college in 1954, that pastoral relationship changed to a peer relationship. (He even asked me to tutor him in Quaker history.) On his first day as president, Milo called me to his office and said, "Arthur, what do we do now?"

Milo came to the presidency at a difficult period in the school's history. Enrollment was low. Loyalties were still divided between Portland Bible Institute and the Quaker college. (Ross himself was an alumnus of PBI.) But a number of yearly meeting leaders were convinced that the yearly meeting should more strongly support its own liberal arts college. These leaders included Walter Lee, Denver Headrick, Allen Hadley, Frank and Genevieve Cole, and the general superintendent, Dean Gregory (who at the behest of the college trustees, had traveled to New Hampshire to invite me — soon to be awarded a doctorate from Boston University — to come teach at my alma mater). I believed this to be God's will for me and began a professorial career at the college in 1953, teaching courses in philosophy, Bible, and religion, with a short stint as dean.

As college president, Milo again excelled as a visionary, a nurturer, and an enabler. Faculty felt supported by him. He drew our hearts and minds into his vision for a strong Christ-centered college. Together — with constituency support and under God's leading — we succeeded.

As noted in Ralph Beebe's anniversary volume, *A Heritage to Honor, a Future to Fulfill, 1891-1991*, Milo made friends with presidents of area colleges and other Quaker schools and gained insights from them (p. 73). He boldly proposed building plans. He increased faculty salaries and added staff. And in many ways he turned pessimism into optimism. He asked Kenneth Williams and me to prepare a status report in a quest to obtain important official accreditation. It worked! We were officially granted accreditation by the Northwest Association in 1959. What a boost that was! Milo raised funds from donors small and large. He incurred debts and erased debts. He inspired faculty and students. Increasing numbers of students came to receive a Christ-centered, liberal arts education. Milo and his associates put George Fox back on a firm foundation to continue its educational ministry. I am grateful to God for Milo's labors, and for his nurturing friendship.

Preface

A Present Generation Hero

Dr. Milo Ross, President of George Fox University, 1954-1969

BY DENNIS HAGEN

*I*N SEPTEMBER, 1980, my son Tim received a book as he was promoted from his Sunday school class. It was Marie Haines's book, *Brave Rebels* (Barclay Press, 1972).

As I read this book about Quaker heroes from the last three centuries, I wondered if Quakers produce heroes of this magnitude in the present generation. After reading about George Fox, Margaret Askew Fell Fox, William Penn, John Woolman, Elizabeth Fry, Elias Hicks, Joseph John Gurney, and Levi Coffin, I was interested that the book closed with persons who lived into the twentieth century.

The first was Hannah Whitall Smith (1832-1911) whose book, *The Christian's Secret of a Happy Life*, provided a view of life as one of joy rather than gloom. It was well received as two million copies were printed, and it has been translated into many languages. She was one of the famous holiness preachers and wrote during the great evangelistic movement among Quakers at the close of the nineteenth century.

Amos Kenworthy (1831-1911) claimed he worked for wages only one month of his adult life, relying on his preaching ministry to sustain his living for himself and his wife and his daughter. He did, however, augment his early ministry by making brooms when he had free time, thus becoming known as the preacher and broom maker. Marie Haines calls him "one of the finest revivalists of the great evangelistic awakening of the Friends church." He was an itinerant preacher who spoke in Friends communities in America as well as meetings in Canada, England, Iceland, and Wales. He had the gift of discernment, miraculously proclaiming through the Holy Spirit what people were thinking in the meeting house where he worshiped. As people witnessed his gift, many were led to salvation.

The publisher of Marie's book, Harlow Ankeny, so eloquently states, "But this question comes to me: one, two, or three hundred years from now, (should our Lord tarry so long), could another writer create a similar volume of biographies on present day Quakers and entitle it *Brave Rebels*? Let us pray it could be done. May these stories ignite a flame in some reader to become, in the best sense of the term, a *brave rebel* in our generation. Perhaps to this purpose we should dedicate this book."

Certainly there are ministers, writers, and educators around the world who deserve recognition for their ministry in the Friends tradition. This book is about one of these, most widely known for his college presidency, but who was first a preacher, church planter, and radio evangelist. To the Quakers of the Pacific Northwest, he certainly belongs in the tradition of Marie Haines's brave rebels.

*I*N 1991 I began researching Milo's life. The Murdock Learning Resource Center at George Fox University houses the archives for both the University and Northwest Yearly Meeting of Friends Church. There was a plethora of materials to read and enjoy. (Visit www.barclaypress.com/Ross for more information about research.)

My reading of all the documents was followed by a period of contemplation about how to use the available material. I wanted to find a way for the documents to breathe with life and excitement. And I didn't want duplication of material already published.

Ralph Beebe has written two histories of the college that include the presidency of Milo Ross. His first book on the subject was *A Garden of the Lord: A History of Oregon Yearly Meeting of Friends Church.* Chapter 6 of this book is entitled "Quaker Education in the Northwest." There is a fifteen-page description of Milo's leadership as president of George Fox College in the fourth part of this chapter (p. 145-162). His second book, *A Heritage to Honor, A Future to Fulfill: George Fox College, 1891-1991,* was written in 1991. It is a much longer and deeper treatment of the Ross presidency, including personnel, buildings, administrative decisions, benefactors, accreditation, finances, and growth.

One of the things I found in the archives was a 450-page typed manuscript identified as "A Mid-Century History of George Fox College" by Milo Ross. Within those pages I saw a window into Milo's mind and heart that needed to be shared. Milo's passion for the college and the Friends Church makes this book something more significant than institutional history. Milo tells a story of determination, perseverance, and relationships. His unvarnished reflection on the challenges and accomplishments experienced at George Fox College between 1954 and 1969 create a pleasant mix of personal story along with educational philosophy and organizational leadership. Publishing Milo's own words became my way to avoid duplication and to create access to this example of Quaker leadership.

O N THURSDAY, September 20, 1979, the local paper declared, "Milo C. Ross, former George Fox College president for fourteen years and a Newberg, Northwest, and national religious educational leader, died on Thursday, September 13, 1979, in Medford (Oregon). He was sixty-eight years old."

Jack Willcuts, superintendent of Northwest Yearly Meeting of Friends, was quoted by the paper as saying, "Gifted with unusual imagination, resourcefulness, vision, and faith, his creative spirit, mind, and heart found expression in many paths of service. His always-positive and courageous leadership shaped the destiny of Northwest Yearly Meeting of Friends, George Fox College, and the lives of young people, collegians, pastors, and his peers across the years of his active life."

Milo's professional life began in 1933 as a pastor at the Rosedale Friends Church in the countryside near Salem, Oregon. Under this young pastor, the church thrived. In 1936, Milo and his wife Helen moved to Greenleaf, Idaho, home of the largest Quaker church in the Northwest. Some of the young people in his congregation were to become significant leaders in Northwest Yearly Meeting. They remember his unusual leadership as their pastor. In 1942, Milo left the church at Greenleaf and went to southern Oregon to open a new church. Actually he planted two churches, one in Medford and the other in Talent. He limited himself to the Medford area when George Bales was called to be the pastor at Talent in 1943.

Milo launched the church in Medford with only his own family, but when he left in 1949, there were ninety-six regular attendees and a new church building. He held a union card with the local carpenters unions over the years and his carpentry skill was brought to bear, not only in Medford, but also in Seattle where he pastored from 1949 to 1953. He modernized the church building there while caring for his children and his wife, Helen, who became critically ill. Her illness forced him to leave the ministry and take her to Salem which was her childhood home as well as his.

He became a postman for part of that year and he also built a home for Helen. It was there that he was contacted to become admissions director for George Fox College in February of 1954. The college had been without a president for two years and Milo was offered this position later that spring, being installed as president in June. He had begun a radio ministry in August of 1953, and the college allowed him to continue this ministry when he became president. However, as his college responsibilities grew, the Board of Trustees felt they had to ask Milo to give up this ministry.

Helen died in the fall of 1954 and Milo married Alice Wheeler in 1955. Alice was serving the college as a nurse after she lost her husband in a shooting accident on the mission field in 1947.

While Milo was president, the college grew from 98 students in 1954 to 419 in 1969. The college was unaccredited and in danger of closing when he was hired, and he is seen as the major force in taking it through the arduous process of both the Northwest regional accreditation and the Oregon state teacher preparation accreditation — and thus its revitalization. Following his retirement as president, he became the chancellor of the Associated Christian Colleges of Oregon for three years. In 1970, he joined the Reedwood Friends Church ministerial team in Portland, which he served part-time until his death. He also served the George Fox College Foundation in an effort to build the college endowment after he left active college work.

This overview of Milo's life reveals how he gave himself wholeheartedly to the life of the Friends church and the college. However, it is important that we grasp the personal side of Milo. It is to his closest associates that we turn to see how he affected people in his years as a pastor and as a college president.

WHILE HE was at Greenleaf, one of his students was Wayne Roberts who became a Medford physician. Wayne said of him, "Milo was an enabler…a helper…he always made people look good, overlooking faults, immaturity, weaknesses — finding something positive and commendable in us all….He lived the creed, 'Do good to all men, especially to them that are of the household of faith' (Galatians 6:10). He was a role model for us all. I can remember that he preached about holiness which made it seem practical and not magical. He preached about peace and reinforced my family significantly. He had confidence in young people, even when we didn't measure up to that confidence. Milo understood what loyalty was made of and the meaning of Christian covenant. Milo stressed discernment, teaching elders to nurture the gifts of the young. As a result of his efforts, I think several elders spoke to me, encouraging me to be faithful to the Lord's callings and urging me to give my testimony or to share a ministry as the way opened."

Joan Logan was twelve years old when she attended vacation Bible school sponsored by Medford Friends. She kept a personal journal over the years and wrote to Alice just after hearing of Milo's death. She shared her journal entry from the following day, remembering her close tie to Milo as her pastor.

"Milo wasn't one to demand perfection or even excellence for that matter. The needs of the new church were such that he had to utilize whatever limited talents were available. Take music, for example. I soon found myself in the role of church pianist, often accompanying with one hand only on the melody line of hymns I didn't know. When I goofed up too badly, Milo would kindly say, 'Let's start that one over.' Milo always gave people permission to start over and retain their dignity at the same time. I guess that all in all, my relationship with Milo has as its essence the incredible security of being loved and accepted just as I am, and of being believed in, regardless of lapses and limitations."

Virginia Millage met Milo when she was a teenager in Talent a few miles from Medford. She was converted under Milo's ministry in 1948. She relates that he became a beloved father to her and remained so through the years.

Two George Fox College students wrote biographies of Milo Ross as college assignments. Calvin Russell's paper was written in 1980 for the History and Doctrine of Friends class taught by Dr. Arthur Roberts. Allison Kingsley wrote her biography as an Intensified Studies project for Dr. Lee Nash in 1983. Allison found many church and college staff members who talked about the personality traits of Milo Ross. Following are excerpts from her paper, "President Milo Ross: Sower of Hope."

"Ross was a man who never saw the negative side of anything," said Charles Beals, a Quaker minister. When the college was at one of its lowest points in his early presidency, Beals said to his wife, "It's *so* refreshing to hear the good side of things at long last." Allison calls this trait of Milo's *eternal optimism.*

The traits of active imagination and adaptability were stated by college professor Dr. Arthur Roberts who said, "Milo was able to image the future so that people lived in anticipation of it and worked toward it. He was genuinely an open kind of person. It's as if the boundaries of his soul weren't so fixed that he couldn't adapt and be the person necessary to fit the circumstances or meet the particular need."

Those who worked in the administration at George Fox had comments about Milo's leadership related to teamwork. Former business manager Frank Cole said, "You knew he was the boss, yet you didn't feel tied down. He gave you the freedom to carry your responsibilities as you saw fit."

Kenneth Williams served in many capacities when the school was small in the 1950s. He said he remembers Milo telling him, "If you have to make a decision and it's the wrong decision, I'll rap your knuckles in private, but in public, I'll stand up for you 100 per-cent." As a former Dean of Students, Kenneth said that Milo "was secure in himself to celebrate the creativity in others."

Allison summarized her paper by stating, "In uplifting oth-ers, Ross did not put himself down, but rather focused away from himself entirely. This is precisely what frees a person to be a true servant. He had pride in his own abilities, as every leader must, but it was not a pride which craved prestige or a sense of superiority. Ross was an exceptional example of a servant leader."

One of the traits of leadership required of a college president is the ability to bring a group to consensus. Frank Cole stated, "President Ross was that way intuitively." Kenneth Williams added, "Milo was always seeing if we could work something out together. It was a beautiful relationship to work with." Bible professor Paul Mills said, "I never worked with anyone I thought was more fair, or more fun."

Milo's servant leadership cannot be seen more clearly than by the relationship he had with his secretary, Gwen Winters. When she was asked how she liked working for the president as her boss, she replied, "As a boss? I never considered him a boss. We just worked together."

Milo began his study of oratory in a debate club in high school. For one to say he had the gift of oratory may be an exaggeration, but he certainly was one of the better speakers of his day. His long-time acquaintance, Jack Willcuts, told the story of an invitation for the two of them to be at a meeting in McMinnville to consider the merger of Newberg and McMinnville high schools, which were only fifteen miles apart.

Jack went as a member of the school board from Newberg in favor and Milo represented the opposing position. Milo came to the meeting late due to a slow plane from New York. As he arrived, he saw Jack and said, "What is this, Jack? I just got in from New York and haven't had a chance to learn what this is all about." Before Jack could reply, Milo was asked to present his position. He began by speaking about the ability of Oregonians to resolve issues in the spirit of openness, not referring to the issue at hand. His speech received good applause and the McMinnville representative declined the opportunity to speak in response. The creative ability to entertain an audience with a sense of authority with no preparation was evident that day. Years of preaching in all kinds of settings provided a great backdrop for this unusual circumstance.

To summarize all that these acquaintances have said would be to recognize that Milo Clifton Ross developed personal leadership traits which had great impact on his fellow Quakers. With his vision and gifts, he will be remembered for his ability to be kind to people in all situations. He was approachable by the least staff person or parishioner as much as he was by the greatest benefactor or titled colleague. The heritage of this one life is passed on to all of us who remain. Might we be as focused in our ministry and as open to the needs of every person we meet, regardless of their title, rank, or position in life.

MILO ROSS was the eighth president of George Fox College. The following list contains two points of interest: (1) the gaps where no president is named, and (2) the long tenures of three presidents — Newlin, Pennington, and Ross.

1881 – 1900: Thomas Newlin
1900 – 1907: Henry McGrew
1907 – 1910: W. Irving Kelsey
1911 – 1941: Levi Pennington
1941 – 1947: Emmett Gulley
1947 – 1950: Gervais Carey
1950 – 1952: Paul Parker
1954 – 1969: Milo Ross

The college had no president from 1952 to 1954. During this time the school's presidential responsibilities were cared for by the Administrative Committee made up of Dean Donald McNichols, Professor Paul Mills, and Business Manager Harlow Ankeny.

It is interesting to look in on the Board of Trustees during this critical time. Faithful California Quaker leader T. Eugene Coffin's name came into the board discussion. Minutes of the September 25, 1953, trustees meeting reveal that board chair, Ivan Adams, was instructed to write to Eugene about his availability. His name surfaces in the October, November, and December board minutes. But by December 30, a board minute from the Executive Committee reads, "It was reported that T. Eugene Coffin was out of the picture."

The Executive Committee of the Board of Trustees had a time of fervent prayer following this report and a recommendation was then made that the board ask Charles Beals, a Pacific Northwest pastor, to consider the presidency. Again, Ivan Adams was selected to make the contact. After some deliberation, Charles declined the offer, according to the February 5 minutes, as he wanted to stay in the pastorate. At this meeting trustee Dr. John Brougher suggested that the board may need to look outside the Quaker church for a president. Dean Gregory, the general superintendent of Oregon Yearly Meeting, felt that the yearly meeting would accept a non-Quaker if they found the right individual. Interestingly, Milo Ross was suggested by the Administrative Committee of the college to possibly be a full time field representative for student contacts and to make calls for the Living Endowment program. A week later, on February 12, Milo was hired for three months from March 1 to June 1 to be the field representative at a salary of $300 a month, plus expenses.

Board minutes record the exploration of various names to serve as president, but no strong candidate was emerging. It was suggested that Milo Ross should be added to the list of presidential candidates and at the March 11 meeting Ivan Adams was asked to contact Milo about being considered as a presidential candidate.

The board reacted very quickly on the possibility of Milo's candidacy. An Executive Committee meeting was held only five days later on March 16. Ivan Adams, Fred Baker, and J. Emil Swanson were there representing the Board of Trustees. The Administrative Committee as well as Superintendent Dean Gregory were also there with presidential candidate, Milo Ross.

Superintendent Dean Gregory led in prayer. The group began to discuss how they might secure Milo Ross as president of George Fox College. Finally, the Executive Committee decided to recommend to the Board of Trustees at the special called board meeting on March 26 that a call be extended to Milo Ross to become president. Dr. John Brougher made the motion that Milo C. Ross be secured as president of George Fox College. Bob Nordyke seconded the motion and the vote was unanimous.

*I*T HAS BEEN my privilege to participate in the George Fox College dream, first as an assistant, then as an associate and finally as a full professor of music. I was also the Chair of the Fine Arts Department. I served under Milo's leadership and witnessed many of the miracles of God's faithfulness to George Fox University. God's blessings have continued to flow through my family as my children (three sons and one daughter) have all graduated from George Fox University.

My wife, Janet, served part-time at the college as assistant professor in elementary music education, voice, and string bass. Eric graduated in 1985 and received an MBA degree from Willamette University. He is a former Tektronix financial officer and is currently CFO of Matco Tool Company located in Stow, Ohio. Pam graduate in 1986 and received an MA degree from Western Evangelical Seminary (now George Fox Evangelical Seminary). She is married to George Fox graduate Gayle Beebe, president of Westmont College. Tim graduated in 1989 and earned his PhD from University of California at Santa Barbara, LLD from University of Virginia, and practices law in Palo Alto, California. Jon graduated in 1991 and received an MBA degree from University of California at Los Angeles. He is vice president of operations for Custom Decorators in Tigard, Oregon.

We have received so much because of the fine training that has allowed our children to become Christian leaders in their professions. We feel very thankful for George Fox University.

Dennis Hagen
professor of music 1964-2003

Introduction

*I*N MY READING of the current histories of American educational institutions, I have noted three classifications: the first is autobiographical, or essays built around the administration of one individual; the second is more objective, having the advantage of an author more removed both by person and time, such as an alumnus; and the third may be characterized by an austere professionalism, sometimes even hostile, but putting the college or university in perspective in the total scene through the eyes of an "outsider." Some are topical, others chronological. Still others come to grips with major philosophical problems of the modern milieu, showing the contribution of the president and peers to the totality of higher education. I have enjoyed the ones — although whimsical on occasion — which demonstrate the types dealing only with impersonal programs, aims, and goals, and the technical "educationese" which, to me at least, can become overpoweringly boring!

All, however, are concerned with "great" institutions — those having attained prominence and prestige over a period of many auspicious and fruitful years, or those which by novelty or experimentation or flamboyance or sudden wealth or recognized integrity have come to their zenith either as new colleges or after years of struggle, mediocrity, and poverty. To assume that recording what I know of the recent history of George Fox College, the "little sister" in a fine family of Quaker schools, can make any important contribution to the already over-weighted bookshelves, is doubtless open to successful contradiction! Were it not that someone must take up the task, and I admit to being the only person who knows many of the intimate details, I would refuse most strenuously. In fact, I have resisted any previous suggestions.

But a combination of providential circumstances has conspired to force me to start the assignment, even if, like Saint Luke in his Acts of the Apostles, I never come to a concluding chapter. Esteemed members of the Board of Trustees of George Fox College have strongly insisted that the task be undertaken while the exciting details of recent developments are still fresh in our memories and vital statistics and supporting evidence are still readily available. Only now in 1968, after fourteen years in the presidency, have time, finance, and assistance all been propitiously granted at the same time, so that I feel free and more capable to accomplish the task.

I begin the project knowing full well that the term "great" cannot be used in characterizing George Fox College, or its history under its previous name — Pacific College. Both honesty and modesty forbid it. A school with a mission, with integrity, Christian, Quaker, evangelical (in its modern, Protestant meaning) — yes. Poor, struggling with many "ups and downs" (mainly downs!) — yes. Without great resources, without major support, boasting few of the "high and mighty," with "angels" counted on the fingers of one hand — yes. For most of its seventy-six years lacking in adequate buildings, short of properties, thin in the roster of doctorates, and woefully slim in library resources, equipment, and facilities — yes. But great? No!

Admitting these serious qualifications and restrictions, I place myself firmly and unequivocally in the position of one who is eternally in debt to all who have gone before — to all of my predecessor presidents, and especially to Dr. Levi T. Pennington who led Pacific College for thirty years; to all of the loyal, sacrificial, and able professors who labored over the years, often on low salaries and without benefits; to every faithful supporter and donor — trustees, parents, concerned Friends, and townspeople who kept the doors open when it would have been far simpler and certainly easier to close them forever.

We will eschew odious contrasts and comparisons. We shall shun the ever-present temptation to build recent success on former inadequacy, or speak of "stronger" faculty, or "larger" this or that, or the present in far more glowing terms than former years. Rather, let us admit to a desperation coming to an exploding head in the early 1950s which necessitated a series of dramatic—almost traumatic—policies, which if not implemented when they were would have resulted in the closing of the school. Under God, taken boldly and with great faith and foresight, they have since proved to be the salvation of the "good old Quaker college."

Nothing which is written should be construed in a light disparaging to the character or policies of any. Whenever possible, and there will be many instances, full credit is meant to be given to the earnest people within the alumni association and without, within the Friends Church and without, within the business community and without, who have made it possible for George Fox College to rise, phoenix-like, from its own ashes. The analyses of attitudes and conditions are my own responsibility.

Rather, let us align ourselves with that group of God-fearing people who can make a parody on Napoleon's famous words, "An army marches on its stomach," by saying, "A Christian enterprise goes forward on its knees!" For a college, and especially one under the governance of a Christian denomination, is a unique institution.

True, she is a daughter of the church, but she differs ever so greatly from all her sisters and brothers in the Christian family. They all have their special tasks: for one, it is evangelism, to another it is social service, to a third it is extension into other lands and cultures, or a mixing of all. But in this, they all have a common source of nurture—prayer and the resultant divine blessing are their daily food. I am convinced after these years of experience and observation that there is an appalling body of ignorance shared by all concerned. The church, by and large, has allowed itself to accept a non-biblical thesis in setting up a list of priorities for consecration, support, and general emphasis, and in the ascending ladder of importance a church college finds itself near the bottom. The college, meanwhile, accommodating itself to its own disenfranchisement, puts its feet under other tables. All too often, the church and the college, instead of being complementary and interdependent, find themselves at odds on an important roster of items, from theology to social patterns to stewardship.

It is the theme of this book to show that George Fox College is all that it claims to be: that it is the evangelical Quaker college of the West, that the church and the college can and do have confidence in each other and sustain each other, that God answers the prayers of his people, and that modern-day miracles are the result.

This history is personal and subjective. It may be the province of a more able chronicler in the future, who by virtue of greater insight and from the vantage point of years to come, to assess whatever may be of lasting value. It will not be profound. Owing to my own mental and philosophical limitations, it will emerge more casual, chatty, and commonplace than most books of like theme.

But in light of all of the disclaimers, I have a *concern* to write the saga of George Fox College! I have been a close observer and for much of the time, an active participant in those scenes. They have become a part of my life. Many of the persons named are my closest friends. When I recall and dream and plan, even in times of reverie or during the night, I have developed a kind of inner compulsion which compels me to put down, at the earliest moment, episode followed by episode. I am like a race horse eager to run, if not to win. And where else could be a better place than in these congenial surroundings enveloped by the serenity of the Sea of Galilee where the Lord Jesus spoke and worked, all made possible to Alice and me by the generous and willing cooperation of my friends on the college board?

Milo Ross
while on sabbatical in Tiberius, Israel, 1968

Chapter one

Raison D'être

I WOULD MAKE this the best evangelical Quaker college anywhere. It will be no easy task, demanding blood, sweat, and toil
from all of you, and especially you. As I have been speaking before
just such groups as this across the country, my theme is *image*. What
is your image? What has it been? What do you wish it to be? I am
concerned that George Fox not be only another pea in the pod."
And to a polite, but spontaneous, round of applause, he sat down
on a front chair.

The speaker was Dr. Thomas E. Jones, president emeritus of
Earlham College, former president of Fisk University in Nashville,
Tennessee, and currently assigned by the Association of American
Colleges as an administrative consultant. He had concluded his
major talk before a called meeting of our Board of Trustees, sitting
as we did in those days in old Room 14 of Wood-Mar Hall. The time
was late winter, 1958, and he had come in answer to my invitation
as part of a tour to the Northwest which included Pacific Lutheran
College, Reed College, and Lewis and Clark College, and for which
he charged us only the per diem rate—no travel or other expenses.
It was the best $150 we ever spent.

He was better than I had hoped. He was bigger than life. He
talked to members of the student body, spoke to the monthly meeting of the Ladies' Auxiliary, and visited classes. And now he had
conferred for a full day with the trustees, setting them off into little

groups, taking on questions in a spirited two-hour-long period in the afternoon, only to finish with a charge to be ourselves and at the same time, unique.

What he uncovered was not altogether pleasing. There was much which could not be complimented. It would be a long, hard road to go. Out of that conference we increased the number of trustees from fifteen to thirty, reorganized the group into meaningful committees with counterparts in the administration and faculty, and created a more viable administrative committee composed of the president and the three deans—faculty, administration, and students. But of all the stimulus coming out of those days, I now concede after ten years, the most significant concept for the future life and success of the college was *image*.

*I*MAGE may have become passé in some circles, but even if its use has rendered it shopworn, being popularized by Tom Jones during those years accomplished a much-needed service to sharpen up American higher education; to jerk lackadaisical presidents and faculties out of their somnolence; and to inspire excellence, alumni cooperation, appeals, and development drives on hundreds of campuses. It was what I had been hearing in the smoky halls and hotel rooms of educational conventions, and the theme was especially pronounced at the conferences of the Council for the Advancement of Small Colleges, to which Jones was an adviser and with which George Fox had aligned itself. It was what I wanted the other trustees to hear. He had lighted the fuse and they were burning already!

Upon this inspiration I researched and wrote a policy paper entitled, "The George Fox College Image." Its theme was to establish a sound educational theory based on the teachings of George Fox himself and to couple this with modern practice. It came to be widely read and quoted.

The route of discovery is both general and specific. It is a part of the total Christian ethic—theological, philosophical, and practical. It also has its specific counterpart in the educational theory of George Fox and the first and later Quakers. It is not the province of this book to outline the history of Christian educational thought. I will suggest, however, the reading of Frank E. Gaebelein's lecture, "The Pattern of God's Truth," and Dr. Bernard Ramm's "Toward a Philosophy of Christian Education," first delivered at Whitworth College in Spokane, Washington.

Dr. George H. Moore, in his lecture entitled, "The Christian College in a World of Change," has this to contribute:

> It should be unnecessary to dwell upon the centrality of the Christian world view in discussing the role of the Christian college for our day. As studies from the Danforth Foundation show, in many institutions founded on the Judeo-Christian tradition, the emphasis has changed to the point that Christian influence is either almost completely absent, or peripheral, or spoken of in apologetic terms.

> Dr. Russell Thomas says that at the turn of the century, educational philosophers were suggesting that heaven is no longer our business and that to concentrate on the other world was to stultify our creative thinking as to what we should do to make this life meaningful and worthwhile. The emphasis was to be on the here and now. Thus, no longer could a world view which took in the eternities be the central, unifying force; other centers had to be provided such as democracy, life adjustment, good citizenship, technology or trade, and economic success.

> Is the Christian orientation limiting and antithetical to the liberal arts? My thesis is that it is not limiting and that it does have relevance. For instance, the psychological concept of ego-extension, postulated as being so necessary for a stable and healthy personality, finds its highest fulfillment in the Christian principle—to love God supremely and one's neighbor as oneself. The Christian concept of the nature of man, a being created in the image of God, would seem to have more nobility to it than the concept of man as a cosmic accident, getting his start accidentally from some primordial ooze.

> The Christian concept of truth which finds its ultimate expression in Jesus Christ—truth which can be discovered

and found, which can have some stability to it—would seem to be more rewarding than the concept of truth which is always elusive; something to be sought after, but never really found. The Christian concept of immortality, in which the eternities can be spent in creative endeavor, would seem to be a far broader concept than that held by some humanists—an immortality only of works done during this life which are of such a nature as to live on from generation to generation—a kind of immortality which is not in danger of annihilation as mankind faces the possibility of the destruction of the human race through nuclear fission. It is the Christian who becomes free from the limiting assumption of the positivist who holds that there is no God; free from the bondage of secularism which binds man to the material here and now. Revealed truth must be brought to bear on the whole spectrum of the accumulated knowledge and wisdom of the ages. St. Augustine made the point that those who only know the Bible don't know it as they should; that the liberal arts belong to God; that only interrelatedness of revealed truth to all knowledge can prepare us for the creative role that God intended.

C. S. Lewis in his book, *Surprised by Joy,* alludes to a "comparison between the Sun and the Sun's reflection in a dewdrop. Indeed, in my view, very like it, for I do not think that the resemblance between the Christian and the merely imaginative experience is accidental. I think that all things, in their way, reflect heavenly truth, the imagination not least." The reader may question my use of the quotation without a fuller explanation. The lengthy and detailed subject of Lewis's essay has no great meaning in my present use. I deduce it solely as corollary support to the general concept that all truth is God's truth. And if a college is not a place for the free flow of the imagination, where is such a place to be found?

Friend Lewis Benson, the Germantown historian, has cautioned me about making too much out of George Fox's allusions to education. With that in mind, I can point out several cautious positions. One is that Fox believed in schooling for the children of

Friends, brought on in part by the simple fact that as dissenters, they were refused the otherwise available opportunities of seventeenth-century England. He believed in schooling for both boys and girls. He believed that the classical, liberal concepts of the schools of that day should be tempered by Friends providing "practical" subjects as well. He does not seem to have envisioned the need of higher education for one and all—the English universities could do that. And as referred to later in chapter 5, he did not advocate special training for the ministry.

*I*T WAS LEFT TO George Fox and the early Quakers, perhaps influenced by the writing of Jacob Boehme and Paracelsus, to affirm the "unity of the whole creation." There is no absolute distinction between the sacred and the secular. Secular educators believe that life is secular. Christian educators believe that life is sacred. There is all the difference in the world! Education has real meaning when Christ is the center. History becomes "his story." Mathematics reveals the God of perfect order. Geography becomes a study of a world that God made. In psychology, we look at ourselves and learn to measure up to the perfect Man. In economics, we provide for ourselves and others, as his stewards. The natural sciences teach us that this universe was created and is being directed by his laws. In fact, everything reveals God. This is the heart of the Christian philosophy of education.

This short and incomplete overview of educational theory acquaints us with the considerable body of current thought and writing on the subject, and shows how Christian theory differs from common everyday American educational theory.

The following is taken from my faculty lecture in 1956, entitled, "A Christian College."

> The Christian college is asserting itself in a resurgence of
> vigor and growth which is encouraging to the proponents
> of this important branch of American higher education. Its
> place in the American scene is not new. Harvard College
> was founded at Cambridge, Massachusetts, only sixteen

years after the first settlers arrived in New England. It was established to train the Christian ministry. For two hundred years before public school took its place in our land, the church led the way in education at all levels. But with the western migration and the founding of land grant public institutions, the public school and the state or tax-supported university have assumed much of the leadership in recent years.

Several types of Christian colleges have emerged. Loosely, all are called "Christian," but there are great differences in structure, control, and aim. Originally, all were "church related, " with boards of regents or trustees named by and for the parent denominations which sponsored the institutions. In most instances the primary curricula were designed to train for the ministry, and only to a lesser degree for other callings, and the content of courses themselves was characterized by its creedal values. Nearly all of the original colonial church-controlled colleges have ceased to be operated by churches and are now managed through self-perpetuating boards or the properties were turned to the public. Many others succumbed to poverty, doctrinal difficulties, or shifts in population.

Recently, groups of Christians without regard to denominational lines, or with the inspiration and leadership of a prominent church leader, have founded and are promoting colleges and universities, the growth and success of which have made a significant contribution to spiritual and cultural life. Newer and smaller sects are traversing much the same path now as did the older and larger denominations in providing for their youth the advantages of a guarded education. And, from our view, an equally important trend is found in the assumption on the part of churches, long since having shown little concern for their colleges, of both control and responsibility. This development is especially apparent in the West, where both the increase of population and the growth of church membership have brought new hope and life to erstwhile small and struggling colleges.

We began to believe much of this ourselves! My point is that both our administration and faculty needed to understand the theological and philosophical implications of being in a Christian institution. Dr. Arthur O. Roberts and Dr. George H. Moore have been advocates of these ideas. Dr. Moore has been most vocal, and I consider him to be one of the ablest leaders in the field of Christian higher education.

Now, since his coming in August, 1967, Dr. David Le Shana has picked up the torch. Each professor needs to understand the import and the impact of this raison d'être [reason for existence]. One of our younger professors reflected after hearing Dr. Moore for the first time that he had come through a sister Christian college never having heard the Christian philosophy advanced so pointedly and, furthermore, he did not think that his former professors embraced it. I once asked a principal in one of our Friends academies about the Christian philosophy being presented there, and he answered, "I doubt that we have any. I have never thought about it. We have Christian teachers and we try to have prayer in the classroom." May I counter by claiming that formal Christian education, at any level, is more — infinitely more — than simply hiring church members as instructors and keeping youth out of places of questionable repute. Too long we have settled for too little. I believe in the influence of godly teachers, and we at George Fox believe in social standards consonant with holy living, but a college such as ours can only hope to cope with questing youth when it is philosophically united and vocal. Point one: we teach ourselves. Point two: we present the claims before the next generation. Point three: we endeavor to propagandize others in the constituency — all who will listen and heed.

If this is not to be a book on the history of Christian and Quaker educational theory, it is to be less so on modern American educational theory. But the college authorities must know where we stand, positively and negatively, in the present field of higher education. The thinking of educationalists impinges on us at two critical points.

*T*HE FIRST is the idea of liberal arts today. True, liberal arts may have a noble history. It may have supported the "grandeur that was Rome," leading the way through the Dark Ages up to the blossoming of the Renaissance. It may have given direction to the universities of England, which in turn were the progenitors of our own American colleges. But the complexities of the twentieth century may have left the traditional liberal arts college back in company with the dodo.

With the passing of the Morrill Act over one hundred years ago creating the state agricultural colleges and their growth up to what they are today — great multiversity complexes — is there a tenable position remaining for the liberal arts college? Training of all kinds, if not liberal, is shown to be necessary to prepare students for vocations and professions which are different from, and more complex than the simple older callings, demanding a new and different type of preparation.

The demise of liberal arts colleges has been heralded for many years, from David Starr Jordan to Jacques Barzun. At the same time, longtime specialized or professional schools, most notably colleges of education, are changing over from their older stance to liberal arts institutions. There is great pressure put upon youth to specialize. There are hundreds of technical, vocational, trade, and other schools having only one or a small number of major fields to offer prospective students. Job opportunities in new specialties appear in every industry. As I said in a chapel talk:

> I suggest that we become acquainted with a new science called futurology. It has to do with projections, the world of tomorrow, our environments, our modes, our order or lack of it — in a word, what things will be like in a few years and how to chart our way between now and then.

And again: There are many thrilling fields of service open to Christian youth, but these youth must be trained in many complex ways. Instead of less education, there needs to be more. Not only will there be greater volumes of material to be covered, but the complexity and intensity of learning will be heightened—more language, more science, and I trust more performing arts; more training for adult living in recreation and sports; more appreciation of music; more use of teaching machines.

Although we may have a strong philosophical base for the conduct of our enterprise, and it may be viable and adequate for today's world as far as our own leadership, faculty, and student body are concerned, it is a hard fact that many in America do not accept the idea. There is cutthroat competition. While it is interesting to read of presidential commissions, foundation reports, master plans, et al., which glibly speak of the advantages of a variety of opportunity for youth—the privileges of each to go as far as talent and ambition will take them—it is plain to see that the "tide of the future" if one considers demand and popularity only, is certainly not the little church-related college hidden in the shade of some county seat, but rather great complexes offering an academic smorgasbord. If we believe in Christian liberal arts, in church leadership, in "all truth is God's truth," and are motivated with a divine compulsion to carry on, it goes without saying that it is incumbent upon us to secure as great a following as possible and be adept in giving the opportunity to as great a number of youth as we can find willing and able to come our way. Enlightened self-interest dictates our doing something overt to change the direction of things.

THE SECOND impingement is in the field of teacher training. Philosophical problems are not found only in general education, but also in the specialized area of *how* to teach others to teach, and *what* to teach others to teach. I am not referring to the "three R's" or the subject matter of lower schools, per se; rather I refer to the debate of whether or not it is the province of the private sector to prepare teachers for the public sector.

Additional implications are the rights of the private to prepare for the private, and the position of the public to prepare for the private! The defenders of the public system are many and do not stand or fall by my single word being added. I understand that the private schools were in the same position a century ago. But private higher education—especially Christian or church-related—faces an insidious and often frontal attack at the very point of having any right to offer education majors.

I challenge the enemies of Christian schools on the subject of truth. Genuine advocates for those schools look at their calling as divine. They are compelled to proclaim truth. They take seriously the prophetic words of the Lord Jesus who said, "And when he, the Spirit of Truth is come, he will lead you into all truth." Girded with the sacred edict, they humbly pray that they may be endowed by the Holy Spirit himself and thereafter empowered to carry out the divine commission. In fact, all truth is God's truth. Truth may be beyond our complete understanding. Our *grasp* of it may be relative and partial, but truth *itself* is not relative or partial. The quest of learning, taken from this point of view, is to realize that truth is divine and that it is our task throughout all of this life and the next to change the ratio of partial darkness to one of increasing light.

Christian education is a mission. It cannot be picked up intermittently as an avocation. Rather than abdicating in favor of other educational tenets, Christian educators cannot let down in the face of humanism, relativism, American democratic theory, or any other opposing theory. They must forge ahead in spite of difficulties occasioned by a lack of apprehension of the divine imperative. They believe it is their right and duty to prepare teachers for the public sector because they are loyal, patriotic citizens and their protégés will be the best examples of citizenship. America, and indeed the world, can be served best by the chain of leadership and education.

Christian educators believe that it is their right to prepare teachers for the private sector. This statement may appear redundant, but it needs to be said. The enriching possibilities of "education plus" are found nowhere more valid than in this cumulative position: truth feeding upon truth, divine light upon divine light, openness to openness. If teachers are to be prepared for service in any of the institutions of the church anywhere in the world, it goes without saying that God will be honored if they secure all the formal education they can under the best of Christian influences; for they will need, above and beyond the minimum requirements, these subjects embraced with their intrinsic values. They are more than subjects to be passed by examination and a grade given, they are more than subject matter or even values—they are pearls of divine truth not only to be learned but to be loved and made a part of one's character. And in the framework of teacher training, they are to be passed on. If church institutions are to be all that the church expects of them, there should be intentionality to ensure more than commonplace transmission.

Additionally, subject matter is important to our consideration. Not only does the Christian teacher candidate emerge a better teacher because of the overtones, points of view, and theories consonant with church beliefs which have been gained in a Christian school, but it is our contention that an understanding of the Bible is ideal, if not essential. It is more than literature or history, more than a humane grasp of our heritage. I refer to a reverent appreciation of it as God's written word; that it is his message of love to all mankind; that one can find in its pages the direction to be taken in present-day living; that its precepts, if followed, would solve problems brought on by greed, injustice, evil, war, and all the rest. A teacher who is armed with biblical knowledge and the love of God through Christ is more able to face a class made up of children or youth, whatever difficulties they may be facing, who need love, discipline, security, and direction.

I have no case which can be construed as a polemic against public colleges preparing students for the private sector. May I present, rather, some qualifications to the wholehearted endorsement of the system. It may be to the advantage of young candidates to have some training under public auspices, primarily in the practical application of methods, state law, administration, et cetera. We have much to learn in expertise. Reservations arise, however, at the place where educational theory may be at variance with the ideals of the church, or less than Christian. From a pragmatic position it could be shown that if all candidates for church schools were to take all of their formal education in public schools, there might come a day when church schools would be little different from public schools. The very reason for the existence of church schools is found in the belief that the Christian church owes to itself and to society the transplanting of ideas, ideals, and loves which are inherent in the gospel; which these schools by their very nature in sponsorship, leadership, and commitment are best able to transmit; and which public schools find more difficult to do.

I submit that a Christian college, in its role as a teacher training institution living up to the demands of the Great Teacher, can and should be an ideal and excellent place. Its "end product," the well-equipped Christian teacher candidate, should be an example of the best in American culture whose service as a professional teacher will enhance the educational system.

A quote from Dr. David Myton, our director of teacher training, supports this rationale:

> The search for common values to be taught in American public schools has failed. An acceptable list of these values is more elusive today than it was when the idea was first conceived a century and a quarter ago. The popularity of existentialism, with its emphasis on individualism, has recast the public school's task into assisting in the identification and clarification of values distinctive to each person. More than ever before, public schools must help students develop values which provide meaning and purpose in a pluralistic society.

*I*T MAY BE QUESTIONED how well we have thought out our case, but it cannot be denied that we have been working on it, and we plan to keep on. There is new truth to grasp, new reasoned conclusions to come by, and new ideas to debate. As I have noted, we do not wish to be counted among the colleges which have no unifying philosophy of education, where pious phrases are found only as a part of the Latin on the seal. Our philosophy must be thought through anew and tested constantly. It must live today. It must be understandable to a questioning parent for instance. We owe it to ourselves, and to all others to reduce it to simple terms in the catalog, or so a professor can use it in an address. Students should grasp the ideas, at least by the time they are seniors.

It is so easy to depend on old clichés and mottoes without adapting them either to modern terms or into simple language. Both are essential depending upon the audience addressed. A rehearsal of catch-phrases demonstrates the evaluation of ideas from previous generations to the present.

I quote from "The George Fox College Image":

> To bring these aims and reasons down to our own immediate instance, in all seriousness, we have had to show that we were distinctive, that we had a set of aims and that we were realizing them, that we knew where we were going, and that we promised to have the ability to candidate the type of professors and recruit the type of students which will make these dreams possible into the future. Here again, I believe that we were honest; but the honesty came from faith in God and not trust in man, and what the future holds is in his hands. But we can enhance our present and our future by a clearer delineation and elucidation of the ideas held and advocated by George Fox, the founder of our church, and what elements should be included in the term *Quaker education*. I think it is ideal that we have taken the name "George Fox."

Another statement, taken from "The Role of the Christian College in the Life of the Church," follows:

> George Fox and his conferees developed a bias against the formal training of their day, and eschewed the Church of England program for the preparation of the paid ministry. They developed a thesis which was correct in its thrust that the main dependence of the ministry should be upon the Holy Spirit. But in so stating, they threw the baby out with the bath. These men, replete with the finished educations of Oxford and the Sorbonne, came to depreciate what they already knew and where they received it, and made no adequate provision for succeeding generations. There should have been more theological training, not less. I sincerely believe that this perversion has been the greatest hindrance to the work of the Friends Church, of all of our failures and foibles. We still face major problems in training enough ministers, to say nothing of the quality and extent of ministerial training. This condition is especially acute in areas where there are no Friends colleges, or the colleges are not interested—as we are—in evangelical, Christ-centered, true-to-the-Bible training.

Practically speaking, unless a college comes forward with a cogent, well-thought-out statement of purpose and aim, it cannot expect to appeal to an audience. It may be to advantage to customize the aims for different audiences. Plans for growth in the physical education teaching norm will be couched in different language from the hopes of the Division of Religion and Philosophy trying to underwrite a lecture series on biblical archeology. To show the extent of diversity in approach, the trade slogan often used in college circles is, "To the prospective student we have everything, and to the prospective donor we have nothing!" So it follows that it is to the advantage, and a practical necessity, that a philosophical position must be taken, elucidated, and advertised—all before money can be expected. A college which in craven, furtive desperation demands support for its needs will get nowhere, for it is erroneous to assume that money alone can help such an institution. Money alone becomes a snare unless there is a philosophical foundation of priority and plan. If it is used only to keep ahead of creditors, it ceases to merit the support of provident donors. Ideas first, money second; not the other way around.

Discouragement may arise when the philosophy is agreed upon and nothing happens. One gets very hungry waiting from the cause to the effect. To wait in cloistered isolation depending upon a high-sounding thesis wrapped up in academicese to produce millions of dollars is a mistake of the direst consequences. The statement first, yes; but an audience is to be found — hearers for the word, viewers for the sights. We can speak with sober truth that one of our greatest problems years ago — and still upon us — is that so few people know of George Fox. It was in 1966 that a discerning patron observed in my hearing that "the college is ten years better than most know." A mistaken or distorted image, not to say such low visibility as to have little or no image at all, is to deny the philosophical position, however beautiful or adequate, any value with the general public. But, notwithstanding the impatience of waiting, it is folly to reverse the process. It cannot be money first, then ideas. There will be no money in that case. Again, the reverse — ideas first, money later — is the only route. Money may come, although delayed.

ONE OF THE IMAGES we desired so earnestly to recapture was the one lost from the first generations — that of an evangelical, genuinely Christian college. The statement in itself may sound a bit strained, but, believe it or not, among friend and foe alike that image has been clouded. Candor must admit that it was not too well publicized. Its return into the evangelical fold is a rare miracle of God's providence. A study of the earliest pronouncements will reveal the sound faith of our founding fathers. And if the George Fox College of today and tomorrow is to seek the loyalty and accept the support of patrons and donors now, the main thrust should be, ethically and morally, in the same direction as those who made the first decisions, said the first prayers, paid in the first money.

Not that we are to retrace our steps, but rather let us establish our tack from the earlier set of the sail. It is not only in the interest of integrity, it is practically feasible. Its feasibility comes from the nature of loyalty and support given to a college. Some objects of stewardship, "charities" if you will, are faddish, of the moment. The supporter-donor gives to a crisis need, a catastrophic demand. Church needs are often presented in one year or five year drives, but a college goes on forever — or so we plan. In the words of a famous college president, "The Christian college is one of the most stable institutions known to man." There is true and sobering meaning in the reading of a will with wording such as, "to the college and its assigns forever," or "for these purposes in perpetuity." Even gifts of the moment, while not being forced into the mold of writing or a formal, sacred instrument, carry with them the loyalty of the donor and the confidence in the college which the latter has established.

This is illustrated by the story of William J. and Anna Earhart, a brother and sister from Seattle. They found themselves spiritually distraught with the liberalism of their denomination, and yet these fine elderly people were ardent New Testament pacifists. They had come to assume that liberalism and pacifism went hand in hand, at least in educational circles, with the current generation of youth. They knew from their study of Scripture that the conclusion was not necessarily so. All the same, they were frustrated in thinking that the gospel of our Lord had been encased in this modern mold. It was with joy they picked up one of our catalogs in a public library in Seattle and read our doctrinal statement. They knew what they read. It was in plain English. Their worried question was, did we still stand by our statement?

When they made their first trip to the college, it was our happy privilege to prove to them our pacifist position. Professor Paul Mills met with them, pointing out from the New Testament the basis of our stand. We prepared figures to show the proportion and number of our students who were conscientious objectors, beginning with World War I. We claimed to be the only college anywhere which offered a sociology class entitled, Peace and War. After having shown them the complementary situation between our stated aims and our active program with a bias toward Christian pacifism, they proceeded to name George Fox College as the principal beneficiary in their estates.

Dr. Arthur O. Roberts and alumnus-trustee Floyd E. Bates represented the college at a preliminary conference in Portland where the research authors of the Danforth study, "Church-sponsored Higher Education in the United States," Dr. Manning Pattillo and Dr. Donald McKenzie, brought their tentative findings. Unknown to us, members of the evangelical community had felt that this was a type of college which was not given a fair analysis, so out of friendly private discussions, Dr. Carl F. H. Henry, editor of *Christianity Today*, and Dr. Pattillo called a study group to meet under their aegis in Washington, D. C. This was in August, 1965. I was invited to represent George Fox. I was to learn that in the estimation of these distinguished scholars, George Fox was "in." From our two days of discussion, there emerged a position paper entitled, "An Affirming College," giving to the educational world for the first time a group theological credo. The original appeared in *Christianity Today*, September 10, 1965, "The Affirming College" by Carl F. H. Henry. Dr. Pattillo made additional notes to include in the final edition of the completed study, and our trustees voted to include it in our Administrative and Faculty Handbook:

> The overall purpose of the evangelical college, as a distinct type of institution, is to present the whole truth, with a view to the rational integration of the major fields of learning in the context of the "Judeo-Christian" revelation, and to promote the realization of Christian values in student character.
>
> Its requirement for full-time faculty includes commitment to the institution's announced religious beliefs, and sympathy with its stated purposes; subscription to an essential core of revealed truths; a vital faith in Christ and a reflection of Christian values in personal conduct; and professional

competence as evidenced in academic preparation, teaching effectiveness, and concern for students as persons. Faculty members are expected to make an earnest effort to relate the academic disciplines to their religious commitment.

The institution seeks to influence the contemporary culture and to be involved in it. It stands unapologetically for the Christian faith, seeks to bring the Christian ethic to bear upon the culture, and challenges the prevailing secularism and humanism of our times. It aims to prepare students for creative vocational leadership and constructive community involvement.

The college of this type regards an honest and an ongoing investigation of all fields of knowledge as an obligation which arises from its Christian commitment, and it thus faces the world of learning without fear or suspicion. This reflects itself in a genuine desire to strive for academic excellence. Conflicting religious and philosophical views are objectively presented in the classroom, by reference to adequate primary sources and library materials, and by special lecturers.

The faculty as a true community of Christian scholars is encouraged to produce significant literature in their fields. The teaching of the Bible is considered a necessary element in undergraduate education, with its content related to other liberal arts concerns. The Bible is viewed not merely as an additive but as an integrating force.

The preferred product of the college is a committed Christian. The religious life of the student is cultivated by required chapel services which contribute through the dimension of worship to the total experience of a full college life.

The college aims to bring students to a knowledge that they walk in the grace of God and that by moral obedience they are truly free. Students are encouraged to recognize that the revealed commandments of God are the supreme criteria of the good life and in both their inner life and external conduct to mirror the example of Christ in human relationships.

The special contribution of this type of college to service professions, such as the ministry, teaching, medicine, and social work, is noteworthy. The administrative pattern of this type of college tends to follow that of private colleges generally. Trustees are drawn primarily from the religious constituency served by the college. Religious conviction, as well as business and professional acumen, is an important criterion in their selection.

Colleges of this type, with few exceptions, have small endowments and limited financial resources. They rely heavily upon their own constituency for support. Some receive substantial denominational support, but most depend on gifts from individuals and congregations. These institutions have close relationships with their churches. Their alumni are making a vital contribution to the mainstream of the church in all areas of leadership.

WRITTEN STATEMENTS are important. Living practitioners in the form of dynamic professors are even more so. They go hand in hand. The word "commitment" has a number of uses and is batted about quite freely in today's world. A person who believes in almost anything or any cause is committed. At its lowest form, anyone who stays at one job long enough is committed! But positively, there is a divine calling to which an earnest Christian, responding in the affirmative, becomes committed. It is common to all communions and all times. In this we have affinity with those who consecrate themselves implicitly to follow Jesus of Nazareth. But obedience to a call follows the hearing of that call, and God uses people to sound it. It is one thing to hear the imperious summons to go to a faraway mission field or to preach in America, but what about the professional opportunities afforded by a Christian college? To be more explicit, does God call a person to teach subjects other than Bible? Does he lead into such fields as home economics or public school music or physical education or drama? What about being in food service or serving in maintenance? Where are we when it comes to public relations or fund raising? These are debatable situations and have been the source of concern among pastors and their serious youth. As far as I am concerned, there is no separation between the sacred and the secular. I admit that the church has from ancient times laid its hands upon the ones to preach the gospel formally, and so has the Society of Friends recorded its ministers. But God calls to any and every legitimate field of service, and without a doubt a college, operated to the glory of God, finds all of its divisions and duties within its scope.

In actual practice, though, Friends (or at least Western Friends) have tended to be stratified into some specialties more than others. We tend to have interests or talents or go on to obtain further training in fields such as education, sociology, history, psychology, and religion, while not being attracted so much to economics or physics or instrumental music or art or dramatics or foreign languages. It is well known in our churches that there are few doctors and lawyers among us. Some fields of professional preparation seem to be easy for us, others very difficult.

Some positions are easily filled with qualified candidates, others go begging. Then there are the new and promising fields of service to which few if any seem to be aspiring. I refer to public relations, development, administration, architecture, educational research, professional maintenance, student services, business management, landscaping, publications, and creative writing, to name the first to come to mind. Why is this? Is it because of the greater incidence of certain talents and aptitudes over certain others? Is our church and cultural background different from the average cross-section of the population? Are these special professions hard to come by in other colleges, too? Would there be more response to them and qualification for them if the need were known? Are disparity between our salaries and the demands of extended preparation, and keen competition factors of the problem?

I do not know if there are simple and ready answers to any or all of these questions. They are indicative of the problems of personnel today, and more so for tomorrow. For unless there is a sudden change in these stratified trends, we shall face serious manpower shortages. Recent history of college professionalism suggests that the services within colleges will become more complex and specialized every year. What will be considered absolutely essential in future decades may be unheard-of or only in its infancy today.

I think of past experiences which may illustrate the work of the Spirit. Dr. Gervais Carey was an able advocate of the Friends belief in the New Testament truth that "in Christ there is neither male nor female," and especially that women should be recorded as ministers of the gospel. He knew all of the arguments pro and con but his capsheaf was, "the most convincing proof that God calls women into the Christian ministry is found when a woman testifies and exercises that call."

Oregon Yearly Meeting was debating the issue of whether or not we should enter upon a new foreign field in Bolivia during the 1929 sessions. There was strong feeling on both sides and someone among those who hesitated asked the question about candidates: were there to be found workers called and trained to the work if we were to elect to enter the field? Edward Mott, presiding clerk, responded by answering that the sanctified judgment and leadership of the church is ideally complemented by people willing to accomplish the task. He was assured, he told the yearly meeting, that God would raise up workers. His acquaintance with a number of church youth who were called and who had begun specialized training to go to Latin America made him bold to say that God was working at both ends. In fact, the corporate church would be derelict if opportunities for service were not provided.

In all honesty, today we find that the demands in higher education are so great, the years of preparation so long, exhausting, and costly, and the growth of the college so dramatic, that we are forced to consider the entire field in a new perspective and a larger dimension. Have we been too restrictive in our views and thus youth have not heard of the variety of challenges? Do we have to admit that there are not enough likely candidates forthcoming for some of these fields? Can we look for a better day when the growing needs of the college will be met by a new generation of keen and superbly equipped leaders in a larger variety of disciplines? We devoutly pray that such will be the case.

It is good, though, to count our blessings. Surely there has been progress and we readily admit that God has answered our prayers in many, almost miraculous, ways on many occasions. Most if not all of our faculty consider themselves to be under divine orders. God has met our needs, answered our prayers, given us talented and trained people so often that we are ashamed ever to have doubted his providences.

*E*ARLY IN MY PRESIDENCY at an educational convention, I heard a statement by a dean from Harvard University. He stated that their policy for hiring personnel was to agree on the best person in the field for the position anywhere in the world, then go after them. The principle is a good one and we have put it into effect ever since. A second principle which we have used constantly is one enunciated by Dr. Charles Finney, the founder of Oberlin College: "Pray specifically." Thus, in relation to persons on a college staff, we should pray that we at the college will understand and follow the divine will, that the person whom we desire to come be convinced that it is God's will, and that all the problems will be resolved and difficulties removed. And the plan works in one instance after another.

In the summer of 1955 I was having a terrible time filling out the faculty list. My biggest problem was Spanish. Spanish at that time was offered for two years and barely constituted a half-time load. I say "I" was having difficulties. Those were the days when a president hired and fired, raked leaves, and dusted his own office, and meetings with a department head (what department or head?) to choose a new associate were unheard of. We had debated whether or not to continue offering Spanish, but it boasted comparatively large classes and the yearly meeting Board of Missions felt that it should be maintained at all costs as preparation for candidates for the work in Bolivia.

In late summer, a woman called requesting an interview. She came at the appointed hour and asked if there were any positions open. I answered with some sounds about being a small school, loyal steady staff, nothing left for more salaries. When I asked what she felt capable of doing, her answer was a thriller! "My field is languages. I like English literature, but I can handle others as well." "What others?" "French, German, Spanish, Italian, Greek, Latin, and Hebrew." This was too good to be true. She and her husband had recently moved to Newberg, and although he did not want her to work full time, she hated to allow all of her education and experience to be wasted—a bachelor's and a master's degree, together with a doctorate from the University of Washington. Dr. Cecilia C. Martin has been with us ever since. At first she was only half time, but eventually a full-time professor taking on about anything where there was a gap in language arts—first Spanish, then French, then Greek, then freshman composition. She eventually become chair of the division and in later years taught her first love, English literature. At the time she joined us, Dr. Arthur Roberts held the only doctorate among the faculty. Her addition not only gave considerable strength in her area, but doubled our number of faculty with doctorates. My prayers had been answered exactly.

There was a deeply committed trustee at the time named Kenneth M. Williams. He was a counselor in the Parkrose (Portland) public school system. I had been his pastor when he was in high school in Idaho and had seen him develop into a capable educator. Within a week after contracting Dr. Martin, Dean Donald McNichols had the opportunity to take a position at Seattle Pacific College and there was nothing to do but accept his resignation with as much good grace as I could muster. It was late August and I was desolate. But my mind kept going back to Kenneth. He had administrative experience and I could tell by his opinions and posi-tions that he had an understanding of Christian education.

Would he consider? What about his contract at Parkrose and the ethics of his situation? What about an adequate salary? One by one, issues were resolved. He was given a release from his contract, a called meeting of the board confirmed all that had to be done, and Kenneth was on the job in ten days! Over the eight years that he served the college, he was truly a right-hand man—tireless, sensi-tive, doing his work well and fitting into every job which had to be filled. He was by virtue of his appointment as Dean of the College a working member of the Administrative Committee, but at one time or another he was also a professor of education, registrar, director of teacher training, placement officer, and Dean of Students—often as not concurrently!

In the spring of 1955 one of my dear fellow ministers, Denver Headrick, came to see me about working for the college. He pas-tored the little Maplewood meeting at the time and supplemented his income by selling cars on commission. There was no opening and no money at George Fox. He came again in another few weeks. Perhaps there was something available in the money-raising line—he and I kept talking. He believed God wanted him to work for the college and I had enough confidence in his discernment and sense of obedience to accept him at his word. Out of our prayerful discus-sions, we eventually put him on a contract: one-half time for thirty days at a time!

I may never have made a better selection. What a find! He began to make friends with people. In a few months, the board was so pleased that they asked him to join the staff full time as field representative. He began to read everything he could lay his hands on dealing with the subject. He and I went to every conference open to us. He became acquainted with hundreds of business and foundation executives in Newberg, Portland, and the Pacific coast. He was known on a first-name basis in New York, Chicago, Los

Angeles, and San Francisco. He bridged a gap with the college and the church, being a wise and ethical confidant with me on problems he encountered out in the field. People trusted him. He and I were most harmonious; he knew what needed to be done, we respected each other, there was comradeship in the Spirit.

I recall the morning when he brought his ideas for the George Fox Diamond Jubilee to me. He called me early in my office, and I could tell that he was excited about something. When I came in about nine o'clock, he slapped his knee, put out his hand for a hearty handshake, and exclaimed, "Praise the Lord!" Then he shared that he had been awakened by the Spirit of God at four o'clock that morning and in the next hours the entire program of sustained development had been revealed to him. Every sector of our constituency would be challenged to share in the cost of the celebration. Would not the college be seventy-five years "young" in 1966-67, and might not the drive build up to an auspicious climax at that time? The plan was a natural. He had it in mind and we needed only to refine it, which we did. Almost as excited as he, I took notes, presented them to the next meeting of the Executive Committee, received a tacit endorsement, and we began to work on the master plan in earnest.

When things were rough, Denver simply prayed them through as he grew into the job, being a better person, a more effective representative, and a more knowledgeable advocate of the profession year by year; for development as a profession was growing at the same time.

The board had considered the idea of honoring people in different categories of service, and we eventually implemented a plan and practice for honorary degrees. The alumni have their Alumnus of the Year award, we honored professors as emeriti. But what about significant service rendered by those who do not fit these categories? We came up with the Distinguished Service Award, replete with plaque and citation; and there wasn't a dissenting vote or question when the development committee, unknown to Denver himself, made him its first recipient.

A S WE REFINED and began to apply the "Harvard policy," two vacancies opened up in physical education. We needed a head football coach and director of athletics, and a full-time women's physical education instructor and director of women's athletics. For most, if not all of its years, women's athletics required only a part time position, but the growth of the department and the interests and needs of the young women called for a move to full time. The administration, which at that time was made up of Dr. Moore, Dean Williams, and myself, spent long hours in research and discussion to find the best qualified man and woman for these jobs. We considered numbers of people (primarily alumni), received the counsel of the board, looked into their recommendations, and finally reached consensus on two candidates. Then we went after them and secured them. The first was Earl Craven, who was at that time head football coach and athletic director at William Penn College in Oskaloosa, Iowa.

Our interest in Earl was nothing new. In fact, we had made overtures to him as far back as 1955. There were always two big problems which loomed up for Earl (and rightly so). One was finance and the other was his career. He and Dorothy have three boys and a girl, and our salaries are not very attractive or competitive. Anyone knows, too, that prestige-wise, George Fox is neither Notre Dame or USC—it is, depending on one's viewpoint, either the end of the road or only a step on the ladder upward. But the Lord had been dealing in the Craven family. Earl and Dorothy had fond memories of Twin Rocks and Quaker Hill camps and they longed for the same opportunities for their children. So by adding up a gross salary of athletics and physical education and admissions, we got them "back home" to the far West.

Earl knew how to do his jobs well. A new professionalism, born of years of experience where things had been done right, was in evidence everywhere. Every locker room began to look neater and cleaner, the equipment shone with new paint and polish, and all kinds of gadgets necessary to the game began to appear — made by Earl himself or a crew of his boys. Most of the activities he suggested were reasonable. His budgets and long-range plans were worked out to the minutest detail.

He excelled in candidating personnel. I have never seen a better job. All in all, he established and maintained a record of administrative efficiency which will have set the norm for all of his successors. He established rapport for the college with the right organizations and people.

We had already joined the National Association of Intercollegiate Athletics before he came, and Earl became an officer and committee chair. He led us into the Oregon Collegiate Conference, representing us in its councils in a most competent manner. His connections brought us in contact with the football greats and especially those with a Christian testimony. George Fox organized a chapter of the Fellowship of Christian Athletes. Fund-raising, public relations, banquets, awards — all of these adjuncts in addition to running a program were handled with finesse. He enunciated a very acceptable philosophy in athletics — simply that the intercollegiate activities were the honors program of physical education. In everything he did, he brought a new high standard of activity and leadership. But I was most happy for his concern for the spiritual life and physical safety of his boys. He put himself into the position of a father as well as a coach. Night and day, no matter what the emergency or problem, he was there. The training was tough, but it protected everyone. The equipment, although not the most elaborate, was adequate and bought with an eye to safety. Nothing was allowed to deteriorate.

He ordered the admissions office with the same expertise. The activities of group recruitment were charted months in advance. He understood the concept of development, using his limited staff to the best advantage. He brought all parts of the school life to bear in his appeal to high schoolers. Not everything he did was novel, for many of the good procedures (such as Dean Williams's Future Freshman Day) were already functioning, but he organized the affairs efficiently and tightened things up, especially the scholarship records.

At the same time Earl joined the team, we secured Marjorie Weesner. Her story reveals a different set of providences, but illustrates our general theme of divine leading. Marjorie was no stranger to us, being an alumna and having served part time in the year 1953-54 as women's physical education instructor. Her husband, Harold, was also a graduate. Together they had moved to the greater Chicago area, establishing themselves in their professions as well as church and community. She had advanced to the position of supervisor of girls' physical education for the high schools of Naperville, while he had progressed to being a junior engineer with the bridge department of the Chicago and Northwestern Railway. It was no secret on either side that I wanted her on the faculty and she would like to come — she topped the list.

One after another the many issues and questions were answered by personal interviews and letters — all except the one of Harold's future. Marjorie could change schools with no loss in standing. In fact, to be called to head the program in her alma mater was a distinct recognition. But Harold's specialty in railroading did not offer much hope for advancement anywhere but in Chicago — certainly not Portland or the Northwest. Success in making the adjustment to a pinpointed spot on the map was remote indeed. I told them that I would work on the problem. First I told of the need in the next prayer bulletin. Second, I contacted the executive committee of the board. Did any of them know of a way to help? Dr. Hester did! His service as town mayor had brought connections at the State Highway Commission.

Within hours personal contact was made with the state engineer and we found that openings were available. Harold was hired and began his duties within two weeks, being assigned to the great Marquam Bridge east-side interchange in Portland. Harold's career had been protected and expanded. And, to our amazement, his superior was the engineer who had written one of Harold's tests at Illinois Tech. The entire affair left us all breathless.

There is no doubt about Marjorie's competence. She was the kind of person who would be an asset to any college or university. She represented the college at the highest level. She taught in an excellent fashion while she and her teams won games over many of the colleges and universities of the Northwest. Her leadership on the faculty was one of the strong reasons why we elected to develop a secondary teaching norm in physical education.

Hector Munn was the kind of fellow who was worth waiting for — but one needed patience to wait for him! A graduate of Seattle Pacific College, he had thought for some time that his calling would be missionary medicine. He took specialized courses at both Azusa College and Claremont Graduate Center. He was teaching at a Pasadena city high school when I first contacted him in regard to coming to George Fox. He and Verna felt led or released to come, and he did join our faculty, but none of us could say that he believed very strongly in the eventual success or strength of the school at the time. Although it was a pleasing position and he would be serving the church, to say that here was a life's calling would be too much. He still debated the possibility of the foreign field, but gradually the thought of teaching in a church college became an appealing challenge.

Hector took leave for some long years of study to obtain his doctorate through Oregon State University. We kept up our correspondence. We visited whenever possible. And then the needs of the chemistry department became so great when we made the move to Calder Center that we simply had to have Hector back part time in 1966-67. He responded favorably. Within a few weeks we were offering contracts for 1967-68 and Hector signed on full time. It was during this late period that he wrote something from Corvallis which made all of his extended study and our waiting worthwhile. It went something like this: "It seems to both of us that

God is leading back to George Fox." His doctorate was conferred in 1969.

James Kennison and his wife, Jo, represented the type of people who have a kind of fierce, but almost starry-eyed loyalty to the college. Jim himself had had no previous personal connection until he came onto the faculty, while Jo Hendricks had attended George Fox for a time and had left to finish her bachelor's degree at Asbury College in Kentucky. She was the kind of former student, though, who would write back long letters to the administration at Christmas, enclosing a $50 bill for the general fund. She met Jim at Asbury, they married, and he joined the George Fox fan club. As the years passed, they both taught high school in different parts of the Northwest, sometimes isolated from a church, but all the while their checks for the general fund came in. Eventually, they made the shift to work at the college, he in coaching and she in teaching freshman English.

After two years, he had the opportunity to pursue his doctorate by teaching at Asbury and taking classes at the University of Kentucky. In retrospect, I believe he hoped to get back to George Fox when his doctorate was conferred, but it did not appear propitious at the moment and we had no vacancies. So off he went to an associate professorship at Eastern Washington College at Cheney. He distinguished himself there, was promoted, did some professional writing, and worked on and won a federal grant. However, with all the fine opportunities and assured ladder of advancement, neither of them was ideally happy at Cheney. They felt isolated spiritually and socially and their children needed the security of a church home. They wanted to come back so badly they could taste it. All of their educational bent, all of their commitment, all of their pilgrim trek could lead only to Newberg. They came back in different roles, not that anyone concerned planned it that way, but for two other reasons: we had specialized niches ready for them, and their training and experience gained in the interim had provided them the preparation necessary to assume these new roles. Dr. Jim went into admissions with a secondary assignment as clinical professor in the physical education department. Jo taught drama. It was a happy homecoming for one and all.

ON ONE TRIP to southern California, I visited different alumni, in particular Norval Hadley who was pastoring the Friends church in Azusa. He had a concern for a young couple, Al and Shirley DuRant. At the time, Al was vice principal of a high school in Azusa and carried moonlighting responsibilities at the local junior college. A graduate of Whittier College with a master's degree from Stanford University, he had gone deeper in spiritual things under the ministry of Hadley until he came to question all of his motivations and goals. Was he obeying the Spirit fully? Did he find in his public school regimen the satisfactions he hoped to find in a life work? Was God calling to something more closely attached to the institutional church? It was here that I entered. We needed a Dean of Administration, and it appeared that his experience in public administration would give him some background for comparison and contrast, if nothing more.

Al was a very sensitive and humble Christian brother, wholly bent on doing God's will. He desired nothing more or less than to come to George Fox and make a success of it. He did a most excellent job in many areas. Detail work in his office was outstanding. He perfected our insurance programs. His scholarly bias in favor of the faculty was most commendable, and something which not every keeper of the purse has! He was constantly engaged in community relations — his leadership of the United Fund, his interest in local artists and their shows, and his arrangements for a Cadbury representative to consider the Oregon filberts as a source of supply. But a combination of problems, too big for any one man, conspired to work against his future with us: a budget impossible to meet (which had been put together before he came), lack of rapport with some very discouraged trustees, and the unhappiness of his family made a lucrative offer from a California firm very attractive. His story may serve to teach that everything may not turn out beautifully when a person seeks to do the will of God, but the work of Christian education is advanced by such people, even so.

Dr. George H. Moore was the kind of person around which Christian colleges can be built. A Friends minister, after pastoring in Michigan, Oregon, and Idaho (where he pioneered the work in Homedale), he felt a growing call to serve the church in Christian education. It was at this juncture in his career that he first came to Pacific. It was a tumultuous and difficult period, but even in those early years he showed rare good judgment in seeing the spiritual and academic role of the college, and in demonstrating that the candidating of a strong faculty was to be his forte. He served some years in a California pastorate, then did more study at William Penn College (during which time his doctorate was conferred). He then returned to California where he taught at Biola College. He had a smoldering desire to serve at George Fox again, and I, too, realized more and more that some day our needs and his abilities could be matched. They came together when we needed an academic dean and a director of teacher training.

George had many concerns: the training of truly Christian school teachers, the gathering of a committed Christian faculty, an exhortation to the church of its high calling in regard to higher education, the adequate support of a faculty — all this and more; but his first love was to enunciate the philosophy of Christian higher education. He understood these implications and he exhibited a rare talent in elucidating them. His Doctor of Philosophy degree in education, his service in the pastorates, plus his growing perception and discernment brought him to a position of secure convincement "that our cause is just." He worked tirelessly to put into effect these convictions. When one begins to count the very outstanding faculty whom he prevailed upon to come and stay at George Fox, always against the insidious odds of competition, one is first amazed and then tremendously thankful for such a stalwart person. His battles were not easily won. He would become terribly discouraged, especially when it appeared to him that his ideal of an academic program would be compromised. But let it be known, the college was stronger and more solidly committed to its Christian role with every year of his leadership.

The coming of Dennis Hagen was another interesting case. He grew up in Spokane, Washington, where he graduated from Whitworth College. Greatly interested in instrumental music, he went on to Indiana University, there to take his master's degree and start on his doctorate. He continued his spiritual quest which led him into pastoral work and he decided to pursue his training for the ministry at Western Evangelical Seminary. It was here that he confided his questions and spiritual battles with a number of sincere associates: was he to be a pastor? What about his gifts in music? Was the Lord calling him to Christian education? Professor Gerald Dillon was aware of these discussions, as was Donald Lamm, a student at the seminary and an alumnus of George Fox (then Pacific College). It was during this time that Ernest Lichti of our music faculty became aware of him and recommended that he join us. Dennis chose George Fox because of his belief in its future and he had an opportunity to build a program with us. There was a spirit of growth and optimism and one new step after another has blossomed under his leadership.

One of the most difficult hurdles experienced in the evolution of a music program in the small college is to move from the small quartet and ensemble stage to a full band or orchestra or both. Students come in as freshmen out of thrilling experiences as part of a uniformed marching band, for example, only to find no great number of interested students. Professors despair to find enough balance among various instruments to practice or produce any acceptable music. Music is written for aggregations of instruments of seventy or eighty and certainly not for three trombones and two violas, to say nothing of the ever-present guitars! While one term or semester may reveal a workable combination, the next may not. Further, many high school musicians never expect to carry on in college. So it takes a number of ideal conditions in the faculty and student body of any small college which must mesh together to create a workable enrollment in instrumental music. We know that a professor with less fortitude and imagination than Dennis would have given up the first day of registration, because a pitifully small number signed up. What did he do? He combed the files for any record of musicianship by any student. Then he secured permission to go through the dormitories where it is now told on him that he actually looked under the beds for hidden instruments! He practically compelled students to enroll with him.

He faced many delays and disappointments, but little by little, demonstrating almost superhuman patience and consummate skill, he put together a successful program. His concerts became great drawing cards. For the first time in our history, the *Messiah* was supported by our own full orchestra for the Christmas concert in 1966. The Diamond Jubilee concert, produced and played before a packed-out, enthusiastic audience on June 3, 1967, was without doubt the greatest thing of its kind to be heard in Newberg up to that time. The reputation of the college has grown as a place for music education and a general music center. Students began to choose George Fox over other colleges by reason of its stellar offerings.

Dr. Elver Voth was one of those fellows who was commited to excellence. Professors are no better than their classroom performance, and this was where he shined. Elver rounded out our present science faculty with his specialty in zoology. He graduated from Cascade College, but showed an interest in George Fox mainly because it is his church college. His was a long, hard row to hoe with a family to support and the very strict demands of doctoral studies at Oregon State University. But year by year he completed more of the requirements until September, 1967, when at the age of forty-four, he was awarded the coveted degree. We were so excited with the news when we heard it in Denmark that we simply had to extend our congratulations from there.

The point of his biography which is crucial to this story was the revelation of his commitment which came out in a committee meeting. He was a member of the scholarship committee and he, along with others, was voicing his displeasure because we had been forced to reduce many scholarships for financial reasons, the primary concern being the elimination of the discount to sons and daughters of ministers. This is what he admitted: "I came here to teach PKs and I fear that this move may reduce their number." Here was a consecration to help the church by his willingness, even desire, to identify with pastors, especially those from the mission points and small churches.

The botany department was developed by Dale Orkney, who received his graduate training from the University of Idaho at Moscow. Dale was known for his verbosity in lectures and faculty discussions. He had worked in various laboratory settings, doing research supported by professional associations interested in pursuing greater understanding of science fields. Dale's special interest was the botanical resources of the Pueblo Mountain area in southwest Oregon. He spent many days and weeks gathering plants, often with students who were garnering summer credit for research in the field of botany.

Jerry Friesen joined the faculty in 1966 as the a cappella choir director. Jerry earned his bachelor's degree at Willamette University and attended the University of Oregon for his doctorate in musical arts. He brought the college a spiritual tone through his choral concerts and oratorios. He directed memorable choral and orchestra works such as Handel's *Messiah* and Mendelssohn's *Elijah*. His choir tours included the states of Washington, Oregon, Idaho, Montana, California, and the provinces of Western Canada. He was active and influential in professional music associations and took the choir on a European tour.

Chris Lauinger was hired in 1963 as a music theory teacher. She and her husband Bob were significant in the building of the music department. Chris was a soloist on the flute, and held a performer's certificate from Eastman School of Music. She had a master's degree from Indiana University and many graduate hours in music theory. Bob also had a master's degree from Indiana. The two of them moved to the University of Arizona, where Bob received his doctorate in musical arts. Bob was a soloist on the clarinet and he taught woodwinds, music history, music literature, and music education courses.

David Howard was a graduate of Simpson Bible College and an outstanding performer on the organ. His academic classes included composition, music theory, music improvisation, music appreciation, and electronic music. He played the Balcolm and Vaughan organ that the Ross family had given to the college. David played it regularly for chapel but he also gave full organ recitals. David went on to pursue graduate work at the University of Oregon and Southern Baptist Seminary at Louisville, Kentucky, where he received a doctorate in church music.

Hiring Bob Gilmore brought to the college a specialist in the audiovisual field. Bob was a graduate of Azusa Pacific College, where he got his baccalaureate degree. He also attended American Baptist Seminary of the West for his Master of Divinity degree and the University of Southern California for his Master of Education degree. Bob was fluent in Spanish and served as a teacher as well as administrator of the audiovisual department. His wife, Maurine, became second in command, offering expert assistance to faculty and students. Bob was well known for singing solos, in duets, and with other members of the faculty in male quartets. He also played the piano very well.

Bob's brother Joe began his faculty career in the late 1960s. Joe was a gifted tenor soloist. He was active in the Reedwood Church ministry as a member of the pastoral team. At the college Joe taught applied voice and toured with the choral group, The New Vision Singers. Joe developed the musical theatre program through wonderful performances of opera, *The Magic Flute* by Mozart and

I Pagliacci by Leoncavallo. His groups produced Broadway musicals, including *Carousel*, *Brigadoon*, and *Fiddler on the Roof*. Joe was the traditional tenor soloist for the oratorio *Messiah* by Handel, presented every three years by the choral department.

*T*HERE IS A GROUP or class of people, perhaps more than any one person in particular, which needs visibility. These include those retired from major universities or larger colleges who wish to teach a few hours after retirement. George Fox is not alone in recognizing the great contribution these people make. Their wisdom and experience are most valuable in faculty councils, as well as the prestige they bring to the entire enterprise. Among these are Dr. Victor Morris (University of Oregon) and Davis Woodward and Wallace Kent, from California schools. Pastors also make a distinctive contribution by accepting the opportunities for service offered. I think of Everett Craven and Sheldon Newkirk in this regard.

Frank and Genevieve Cole stand out as people who educated themselves for a second career. Both are alumni of the college and maintained a loyalty over the years. After a career with the post office, Frank took early retirement from the regional office in Seattle. During the early years of his first career, he completed his master's degree. Genevieve took a master's in librarianship at the University of Washington. Thus, they made themselves available for service at the college.

Frank discussed his situation with me on several occasions prior to deciding to come. Being a trustee made him acutely aware of personnel needs, and he first considered an appointment in the field of business only. When contracts were drawn up for both of them, his was part-time in business with the remainder in public relations. Genevieve was hired full time as the assistant librarian. But it was not long until the Dean of Administration position opened which the Executive Committee believed Frank should fill. In order to do so, he took very light loads in teaching and others took over in public relations. By 1968, he was completely out of teaching.

Frank gave himself without stint to his heavy assignments as the Dean of Administration. While his first career with the federal service had prepared him in personnel management and office procedures, he was to find that creating budgets, meeting payroll, financing major buildings, dealing with creditors, and facing the problems of reductions and limitations were of different stuff in a little college. Further, he fell heir to crises which came tumbling in on us by the "tight money" of 1966, so that his gigantic accomplishment was to refinance the entire college. Beginning with the ever-improving budgets of Harvey Campbell and then of Al DuRant, his had been honed to a fine point indeed. All of us in the administration and representing the board alike came to accept his computations and projections at face value. His dealings with our bankers and the governmental officers in Health, Education, and Welfare were of the highest order. The college was held in high esteem because of him.

Genevieve, likewise, made a real contribution — maintaining a fine sense of what a librarian should do and be. She carried a deep concern for the spiritual life of the students who worked with her.

WITH COMPETITION from government, industry, and other universities, the fields of physics and mathematics were especially critical. We simply could not compete for salaries. We had not, until recent years, kept up in equipment. There was no community of scholars such as one would find in a large department. Further, without a full major in physics it was disheartening to have no graduates in that field. At the same time, from an administrative point of view, we wished to offer an adequate program, replete with capable leadership and a good environment for learning. What we did do, we wished to do well. We hoped to draw the best students into the field and then to do right by them. Administratively, we could not engage a full-time person because the classes would be too few and too small.

It was during this time we first knew of Dr. John Brewster. A graduate of Pasadena College and with a doctorate in physics from the University of California at Los Angeles, he had come north to associate himself with the Field Emission Corporation in McMinnville. He had advanced to the position of vice president and director of research, but he was a scholar and scientist who loved to teach undergraduates. Further, as an active and devout Christian layman, he came to think that George Fox was the kind of college with which he wished to associate. He could not break away from Field Emissions for obvious reasons, so a little "moon-lighting" was ideal for us and congenial to him.

Dr. John gave himself untiringly to preparing lists of needed equipment and material so that donors could be challenged to give. His knowledge of professional hardware was the best we could have come across. Some young professors, however capable and challenging and possessing many elements of potential, do not know the manufacturing firms purveying to their special field, nor do they on occasion possess the judgment and wisdom to set out a program of purchases which is acceptable to prospective donors or consonant with the aims of the institution. He had these qualities to a marked degree.

We were thankful for his gracious manner in dealing with his peers. For the first three years of his association, he was the only one who held a doctorate in the sciences. He could have thrown around his weight or condescended to others, but instead he took a supporting role, building up his colleagues in his attitude, and with students and the administration directly. Small colleges could well afford many more like Dr. Brewster!

I CANNOT CONCLUDE this section without referring to Dr. David Le Shana. His name first appeared as a candidate for a vice president or future president at Santiam Lodge in September, 1961. Ivan Adams was leading the workshop, Succession to the Presidency. I had insisted that the trustees come to grips with the question before some crisis arose. What if I were killed, or inca-pacitated accidentally, or suffered a heart attack, or some prob-lem between me and the board dictated my stepping down? The discussion brought forward a list of names of likely scholars and churchmen, none of whom knew they were being considered. The discussion also considered the matter of a more immediate assistant for the president, crisis or no; future academic preparation—what should be the nature of ideal training and experience; and whether or not any should be contacted fairly soon in any way and by whom. Altogether, it proved to be a most productive workshop.

During the intervening years, the list got smaller and David's name loomed larger. In every sense, he dominated our horizon, especially by completing his doctorate and demonstrating leadership in and loyalty to the evangelical cause. No other candidate finally rose to the top in these critical areas of qualification. We kept in touch.

In January, 1967, David let me know that he was terminating his service at First Friends, Long Beach, and that he was praying for divine direction about his future. The pastorate or a position in higher education were the two possibilities. While it seemed ideal to bring him in as a vice president, or in development, our projected budget forced us to hold the line on all personnel other than professors, promising Dean Moore we would honor his needs for teacher training. Thus, if any added persons were to be engaged, they would be clinical professors or director of the cadet program, and not an administrative person. I had to so inform David.

In April, a new factor entered the picture. Dr. Bulgin of the Associated Christian Colleges of Oregon let it be known of his keen desire to have David join us. Dean Moore let me in on the observation. It so impressed Dr. Moore that he came to me with a novel, even startling offer. Why not grant him (Dr. Moore) a year's leave, thus giving David an opening and position? The salary of the one could shift over to the other. That Dr. Moore wished a year away was not surprising. He was most discouraged over trying to build a strong faculty with insufficient funds. He was fatigued. But to make the offer in connection with David also made me realize in what high esteem David was held among my peers. And almost as a joke, I responded, "George, why don't I pull rank on you and I take the year off?" His answer was that he was willing for the counter move, if I would arrange for his leave a year hence.

I brought this before the executive committee. I laid out before them in writing the overall situation as best I could, which stated the general college condition, my hope for travel and respite, Dr. Moore's problems, and the fact that David Le Shana was a distinct possibility. Before the evening was over, I was authorized to phone David immediately—which I did. We brought him to Portland for an interview within forty-eight hours, and conducted a total of four called meetings of the executive committee within two weeks!

He conducted himself to the liking of one and all. Not only was everyone on the committee in full agreement, they were delighted. All who got wind of our interviews and the possibility, both on the board and in the college faculty, responded most favorably. But our evident satisfaction was not the final answer. He was torn between the offer from George Fox and an attractive offer from a larger Christian school in the East. He asked for more time from our competitor. They countered with a more enticing offer. The tension mounted, peaking a full three weeks after our initial meeting.

Through it all, we had the knowledge—perhaps the feeling—that if David were to accept, it would not be the salary (for we were unable to match the competition) but a genuine sense of call. So it was that, at long last, when he summed all of the conflicting pulls and debates which he had gone through concerning his own life's work, he settled on us because he could do no other. George Fox came to mean to him something which is indefinable and all the while actual, an embodiment of sound Quaker education. He wanted to be identified with it. He could throw himself into its future without hesitation. He wanted to carry its banner. He knew that just such a college had to have a future, and he hoped to be a part of it.

David and his wife, Becky, were our guests at all of the commencement affairs, sitting in on the social events, meeting our community and constituents, and he met with the board and marched in the processions. They went back to Long Beach to finish his pastoral duties. His doctorate was granted in August, 1967, just in time for their move north. His broad background in Christian circles, his acquaintance with so many leaders in the field, his awareness of church relations, his qualities of wisdom and leadership for one so young, his dependence on the Lord for direction, his optimism and gracious manner all gave him a most auspicious initiation into the work. I immediately sensed that the college would be in good hands. In fact, as the first year progressed, it became apparent that almost unheard of progress was being made on many fronts. The college forged ahead with its highest enrollment and a superior level of performance in one field after another. If his first months were any indication of the future, our judgment would have been amply rewarded.

WHAT HAVE BEEN set forth as little biographies of professors is representative only and not in the least to be taken as exhaustive. Nor is the list to suggest that others on the faculty demonstrate these qualities to any lesser degree. They have been lifted out to illustrate elements of obedience to the divine calling which are not only in evidence personally and subjectively but which as an administrative policy show our active pursuit of dedicated, highly qualified personnel. The Christian witness of a college can rise no higher than the sum total of its living protagonists, and if a college is truly Christ-centered, the faculty are on the staff not by happenstance, but by the combined policy of board and administration—the formal position of the trustees, honest and wholehearted compliance of leaders on campus, strategies of the dean of faculty, open acceptance of the community of scholars.

Let us turn our attention to innovation, experimentation, and research as they give character to a college.

ONE OF MY rude awakenings as a novice president was the early awareness that little if anything is secure or static on a college campus. I was naive enough at first to think that a college catalog, once "nailed down," was to remain that way for some length of time! How was I to know that every new professor was prone to come forward with new and different courses, or classifications, or numbering? How was I to know that what was on the menu for hungry students—had been for fifty years—was easily shown to be passé, inadequate, and not at all what the best schools were offering? I was soon to find out! The tension concerning proliferation of courses will always be debated. It is simple for an economy-minded trustee to observe that our problems are all caused by too many courses. At the same time, a professor may rightly believe that one specific offering, representing a novel approach to knowledge, may appeal to students, and thus by adjusting to demand, we might be able to hold more students on to graduation or even entice new ones to attend. We carefully reviewed the size and number of classes, major fields, student demands, efficient use of space and equipment, the level of teaching in high schools, the direction of the state system, and the requirements of graduate schools. This state of flux, this academic ferment is an exciting thing. Rather than drawing back from it, from locking the curriculum into a rigid straitjacket, the issues of educational structure are the warp and woof of a college.

This was more than mechanics. We were able to evidence overall a search for the best ways to offer units for learning. We took advice from many sources, leaning heavily on the sparkling new ideas gained at workshops and conventions. The meetings of the Association of American Colleges and Council for the Advancement of Small Colleges, for instance, were exciting in this regard. At one time we brought in a major professor of mathematics from the University of Washington who advised us on the direction which that field should go. Professor F. L. Stetson, the emeritus dean of the School of Education at the University of Oregon, helped us initiate our honors program. Professors at the university's School of Medicine gave us invaluable assistance more than once in developing a stronger offering in premedicine, predentistry, nurses' training, and medical technology. We found that the administration and staff of our sister colleges — Willamette University, Linfield College, Pacific University, University of Portland, and Marylhurst College — were most creative and helpful to give us freely of their wisdom in innovation and experimentation. Dr. Victor T. Morris, dean of the School of Business at the University of Oregon, gave of his time and judgment to advise us in setting up our major in economics and business, eventually coming to teach for us after his retirement. Two extended conferences — one in Vermont on experimentation, and the other nearby in Salem on creativity — stand out in my memory as prime examples which were to affect the direction of much of our thinking for years to come.

Those in leadership must create a climate conducive to experimentation. Fear of change must be removed. Imagination must be allowed full play. Time must be reserved and taken in quiet surroundings to conduct "think tanks" on one thing after another, perhaps free and open and without structure. There were several such times when various groups spent days at isolated retreats — without distraction, relaxed, easy, friendly — to address curriculum change or honors or church relations or finances. I found that it was my position, honor, and joy to lead out in them in order to place myself at the vanguard, to order my affairs by example, and to keep abreast of the latest thinking.

Such a climate is exciting and liberating. Young faculty members are intrigued to join a college community where a reputation of acceptance is known to exist; older professors stay on for years. A reputation thus gained is a cherished jewel. The college comes to be known for its openness to new ideas. It is no longer a stuffy place, slowed down by its own lethargy, wallowing in its morass of ineptitude or bound by its fixations. Ideas spring up from every quarter — from trustees, students, townspeople, and gardeners.

AT THE SAME TIME, the posture of cordiality to innovation makes a school very vulnerable. On one hand, it is possible to tilt off toward a dozen windmills at once. The school can lose its sense of commitment or direction. Too many ideas can result in futile efforts. Change can be forced at a rate that can only result in chaos. Not enough study, time, and preparation may be given to ripen the ideas, not enough "publics" may be involved to make them acceptable. But the risks are worth taking.

On another hand, resistance may develop which says in effect: "We are good enough already." Granted, any community of scholars must believe in what they are doing. But to say that all that has been done—all the techniques, all the groupings of instruction, all the methodology (or any major part)—has been misdirected and ill-advised is a foolish position to take. Taken in the extreme, rigidity can spell doom to an ongoing institution. There must also be an attitude of humility which admits that any one college, however fine its reputation, cannot have all the answers. For whatever the prestige of the past, what sufficed a few short years back may be unacceptable today.

The explosion of knowledge, the overmastering mass of it, and the limitations placed against a small college, force a faculty against the proverbial wall, asking themselves, "What should be taught, and how?" And, "What of the past is relevant for today and tomorrow?" As one philosopher has come to admit, "The question now facing us, for the first time in history, is what *not* to teach."

Out of this milieu, a kind of academic practice emerges. It is weighted heavily to persons of quality. It endeavors to make studied and wise moves, assimilate them, and then exploit them to the full. It builds on limited strength until that strength is no longer limited. It has a healthy respect for the classic past, but has its eyes on the future.

I HAVE ALREADY ALLUDED to the tensions of curricular change. They come not only quantitatively, they stem as seriously from qualitative considerations. They have to do with the intrinsic content of what is taught. Shall liberal arts control the core? If so, which liberal arts? The Roman kind, the medieval, the colonial American, or twentieth century? It goes without saying that we dare not turn back the pages to the past. But what appears to be an ever greater debate is to prove, if not to ourselves then to the general public, the relevance of liberal arts at all. We must not be guilty of corporate rationalization. We should eschew the temptation to justify our position by simply amassing arguments on one side while ignoring all others. But, if one can read the signs of the times with any degree of accuracy, a liberal education is still an ideal academic base for the current-day student, giving balance and (to us, at least) a point of view which the technological American so greatly stands in need. Even from the view of securing employment (which is the view so often adduced by professionals today to substantiate their position on purely technical and scientific preprofessional training), the rapidity of change and increase of scientific knowledge seem to give a greater relevance to the liberal education. The stance of the students of liberal arts is far more negotiable. They can shift. They can "roll with the punches." They are not left to begin all over again. This does not say that the great bulk of educational theory and practice will come to accept what I have presented. There will be more advocates in defense of the multiversities. But the liberal arts college still has a case; perhaps the best case in all its distinguished history. It owes to itself, even so, a serious study of itself and what it purports to accomplish with its students.

How does a college prepare its graduates for technical skills or the variety of professions? What adjustments in an undergraduate program need to be made? What niche can our college fill better, or at least differently from most other colleges? Is there an advantage in emphasizing a particular discipline, or more than one?

Reaching into the past, it can be deduced that the traditional American liberal arts colleges (to lift out our noble predecessors by way of illustration and example) were famous as a group in producing three sets of professionals to lead the society of earlier days—ministers, doctors, and lawyers. We learned several lessons from this fact. One was that whatever the claims of the future and however the curriculum may need to be revised for tomorrow's education, it behooves us to concentrate on the basics first. Ministers, doctors, and attorneys are still essential in today's world. True, no longer does a four-year college offer all of the formal education necessary to these fields of endeavor, but its four years are nonetheless important.

Another lesson was to study the relative success of George Fox in producing graduates for these three professions. We were to find a shocking imbalance here. The number of ministers and missionaries was very satisfactory, relatively speaking. For a school which had been so small, literally dozens of Christian workers had gone out all over the world from the pioneers at Kotzebue, Alaska, before the turn of the century to the most recent class of alumni now attending seminary. In a survey of students in the 1964-65 student body, we found that two-fifths of all those preparing for church vocations for the Friends church were in that student body. All of these data were encouraging, challenging, and sometimes perplexing.

But when it came to the preparation of students to become physicians and attorneys, our record was dismal indeed. The problem was found in two related areas: lack of accreditation and limited undergraduate courses to prepare for professional graduate schools. It was practically impossible for any candidate during the forties and fifties to pass the entrance examinations to medical school. The last to do so and successfully pursue his career was Dr. Wendell Hutchens who graduated from Pacific in 1928. A dentist, Dr. Claude Lewis, after graduating in 1947, later worked his way through the Oregon Dental College. Much the same problem faced prelaw students, but for different reasons. Our curriculum was simply not broad enough to prepare them. (A discovery of this fact was one of the strong arguments used in support of our full-fledged majors in economics and business.) Our findings revealed that the nearest we had come to preparing an attorney since World War I was when Bernard Newby attended Pacific for two years in 1926 and 1927 before transferring to Willamette University, and

Lloyd McClintick had been with us for two semesters in 1946-47 before moving to the College of Idaho. It did not take a team of researchers to report our dismal record! Further, the present generation was bypassing George Fox if they anticipated entering these professions.

As a corollary to these reports, several ministers on the board strongly advocated a full program for the undergraduate education of lawyers from a practical, pragmatic argument. The Friends church, notably in the west, boasted very few attorneys. Attorneys are a good class to have in the church membership for reasons of judgment, their witness, and their financial support. Their paucity is a loss to the church. Therefore, let us work toward creating a new generation of attorneys.

A similar argument was advanced in regard to the medical profession. Statistics show that as a class, physicians earn more than lawyers. And if the college were to grow and eventually find the financial support so necessary to fully undergird its programs and guarantee its continuation into the indefinite future, a new generation of professionals would need to come forth, take leadership, and become part of the support network.

Again, practically speaking, both the church and college would bankrupt themselves if the challenge to church vocations was not matched by consecrated youth entering more lucrative professions. It takes ten stewards to send out one missionary. It takes ten families with average salaries to give minimum support to a pastor. So, if there are few if any practitioners in the leading professions, the kingdom is impoverished in every way. We must begin where we are. We must, now that we are accredited, organize our offerings so that candidates can find an adequate opportunity, be challenged to pursue their full four years with us, take and make an acceptable showing on their entrance examinations, and then demonstrate the acumen and perseverance demanded to eventually earn the coveted laurels.

The plan is working. More medical candidates and aspiring legal minds are now in preparation at George Fox, or in medical or law schools, or have recently graduated from these professional schools than at any similar span of time in our history. Another way of illustrating progress is to say that there are more majors in these fields in the last five years than in the previous fifty.

OUR DISCOVERIES concerning the three major arts professions and what we did to improve the situation is but one adjustment which we needed to make. We began to develop a rationale in regard to modern technologies, the type of formal collegiate experience conceived to assist our graduates to live in the last third of the twentieth century.

The state of Oregon had gone through a comprehensive study of its own projections and we, along with every other institution of higher learning, had our vision expanded. As significant as anything which came out of the study was the method of the study itself; much of it was accomplished voluntarily, without paid staff. I caught an idea and contacted a number of people of distinction who came to serve George Fox in an outstanding way on a research commission.

First, I asked Governor Mark O. Hatfield, who was a trustee, to serve as chair. We met at the capitol and after outlining the problem facing the college we made out a list of other candidates to serve on a research commission. We realized at the outset that much which would come about would need to be done by correspondence or sessions with partial attendance, but agreed that the attempt was worth it. We decided that Governor Hatfield would be called on to preside and to sum up the findings, but that my office would do most of the "leg work."

Next, we invited Dr. Roy C. Lieuallen, Chancellor of Higher Education for the state. His most recent project involved all schools and all types of formal post high school education which gave him a newly-acquired perspective much to be desired. His offices in

Eugene held a great store of the most valuable information which was made available to the Research Commission: data on enrollments, major fields of study, high school projections, population trends, et cetera.

A third member was Gerald Frank of Salem, chair of the State Research and Development Commission, best known for his partnership in the Meier and Frank Company. Having spent a number of years in public service, his main contribution came in the area of Oregon's manpower needs.

Loran Douglas, superintendent of Newberg's school system, gave of his time and understanding, especially in regard to the future education of youth in the surrounding district; how could George Fox provide for a greater number of students to pursue further education while staying at home? What was Newberg's potential in relation to the greater Portland industrial complex? What were the present student demands which were not being easily met?

Gerald Edwards came to be a most valuable member. Having been at Stanford University and Harvard Graduate School of Business, he combined in fine fashion his understanding of what a formal education ought to include with his practical knowledge of Oregon business.

The only member of the alumni association and one who lived outside the state was Dr. Lewis Hoskins, professor at Earlham College. I deemed his knowledge of overseas programs to be invaluable. Although he was unable to attend any meeting personally, no one in our college family knew more about the advantages and mechanics of launching and carrying out programs in international studies, and he turned in a valuable critique for the use of the Governor.

At the first meeting we agreed on a working plan, summed up as follows:

> Each member was to answer in his own mind if George Fox
> should continue as a liberal arts college. If not, or if major

changes were to be suggested, what additions or deletions should be made?

What were the strengths evidenced over the past, and what was our traditional reputation?

What new fields might we enter?

If the college were to specialize, in the light of Oregon man-power needs and what other colleges were offering, what direction should be taken?

These queries were first answered personally, then taken up at called meetings over a period of weeks. We had a full meeting after three months in my office, presided over by Governor Hatfield after which he reported to a called meeting of the executive committee.

There was general agreement that George Fox should maintain its character as a Christian liberal arts college. This in itself was unique. The greatest discussions were over the subject of distinctives. All agreed that a college—in particular, George Fox— should be renowned and famous for something, but the debate was whether we should create something new or take one of our stronger majors and undergird it.

It was recommended that we develop a school of banking. This could grow out of our majors in economics and business with the addition of hosted conferences, research projects and the addition of an eminent faculty, respected in the business community. After conferring with E. C. Sammons, retired president of the First National Bank of Oregon, and Mr. Phillips, senior vice president of the bank, it was concluded that the idea was not sound. There was no need for another school of banking since those educational needs were already met through the American Institute of Bankers' national program. We hoped other avenues of inquiry would be more fruitful.

One basic position was assumed by the Commission: we should capitalize on the type of faculty and caliber of students recruited. We have a demonstrated tradition of compassion and sensitivity to human need. These qualities have shown themselves in the past by the simple fact that a large proportion of our graduates have given themselves to sacrificial callings. There is an awareness today of human need that has caught the idealism of youth, not limited solely to the work of Christian missions — for example, Peace Corps and VISTA. Problems in our cities are crying out for a certain kind of person. "Special education" — designed for the handicapped, for the mentally challenged, for those standing in need of rehabilitation — demands unique programs in teacher training. Social services at both the undergraduate and graduate levels are expanding dramatically on the national scene and require specially-trained personnel. Health, Education, and Welfare grants in the United States and foundation grants for other countries currently tend to be heavily weighted toward these specialities and programs.

All of these types of education can build on what George Fox already offers. None change our character or destroy our uniqueness. One entire session was devoted to these possibilities. The Commission took a serious look at our science facilities and offerings and new factors were enumerated: a new building, the latest equipment, the caliber of faculty, and the performance of students. It was suggested that it might be greatly to our advantage to promote these areas even further. The group deferred to the trustees and faculty to implement whatever might come of these suggestions. Many emphases were discussed other than the broad concepts of social education and training directed toward meeting human needs: primarily adult continuing education, adaptations for business training, and some consideration of foreign programs.

As can be surmised, considerations of the Commission were many and varied, the possibilities brought to light were tremendous, and any one major recommendation could have a leading role in the future success of the college. We shall continue to be greatly in the debt of these gentlemen. George Fox College has its *reasons for being* — raison d'être. The next chapter will honor those who have helped to realize its dream.

Chapter two

Benefactors

"MILO, I'm a heel. I never should have written you like I did. I only wanted to find out if you had enough gumption to come ask for it," (meaning money for a library). So said Gilbert Shambaugh, who had amassed an estate of $1,000,000 in New Mexico real estate, as I met with him in the summer of 1960 in his home on the west bank of the Rio Grande in Albuquerque. I was on the threshold of the greatest opportunity in the history of the college. I knew it, and I had to play it cool. Within the next twenty-four hours, he and his gracious wife, Olive, were to tentatively pledge $250,000 for a library to bear their name, and before the project would be completed they were to increase their contribution to $275,000.

Shambaugh's saga reads like Horatio Alger with flourishes. Orphaned as a lad in Ohio, he went to live with an aunt and uncle. In his teens, Gilbert contracted polio, although no one seemed to know the nature of his debilitating fevers, and after three years in bed he had virtually lost the use of his legs. During early adulthood he got around somewhat with a cane. By the time we met him at the age of seventy-three, he called himself "one-fourth of a man." He was completely paralyzed on his right side. He was a skillful one-hand driver, and at home used a wheel chair.

During the course of a half day, he drove us over much of Albuquerque and Sandia Knolls to the east of the city to show us his properties, and during the hours of driving told us about his life and struggles. He worked his way through Earlham College in Richmond, Indiana, graduating at the age of twenty-seven. He came to teach at Pacific College during World War I, and there he met and fell in love with Miss Olive Johnson, a student, and secretary to President Levi Pennington. They were married in 1920. Years of public school teaching followed during which time Gilbert received his master's degree from the University of Oregon. Eventually moving to Palo Alto, they worked together to get him through his doctorate, and he had the enviable distinction of having been granted the first Doctor of Education degree ever offered by Stanford University. They continued to live in California, but he was never robust.

At the age of fifty-five, with $5,000, they moved to Albuquerque, New Mexico. He developed his specialty there in real estate law and by the time of his death he was recognized by the legal profession and the Spanish-American community alike to be the greatest authority in that field,

Gilbert and Olive exemplify the type of people who had previous connection with Pacific College, only to completely lose contact in subsequent years. To such—alumni and earlier teachers, especially the keen ones—the college had become an embarrassment. They never made a contribution. They never came to alumni meetings. They sent their children to other schools. And I, having attended another university, found that my knowledge of the members of the alumni association was practically nil.

True, I knew that Mrs. Shambaugh was an alumna. I knew that she was an aunt of my secretary, Gwen Winters. When Gwen and Arthur visited the Shambaughs in the summer of 1958, Gilbert and Olive's interest in George Fox College revived. The Shambaughs have stated repeatedly that had it not been for the Winters, the library would never have been built—by the Shambaughs, that is.

So when a surprising letter came from Gilbert on a morning in April, 1960, I went immediately to Gwen for counsel. While visiting the Winters in 1959, Gilbert had picked up the March issue of the George Fox College "Bulletin." The lead article announced the accreditation by the Northwest Association of Secondary and Higher Schools, listing among other recommendations, that the library services should be improved. Gilbert and Olive decided to begin correspondence with me with the thought and hope of leaving a lasting monument at the school where they had first met. I had never received such a letter before and few of its calibre since. He asked all kinds of questions, mostly of a financial nature, about the size and cost of a proposed library and the process of converting properties to a tax exempt benevolent corporation. The questions were so involved and technical we were forced to secure legal advice. I also interviewed the trust officers of two banks and received written opinions from the Portland office of the IRS.

I answered as best I could. Then I waited. In a few days I received a telling reply. The letter read in part: "Dear Dr. Ross, I knew all the answers. I wanted to know if you did" (signed, Gilbert Shambaugh). The letters came and went through the spring and early summer, and the executive committee met and passed crisis after crisis. When trustees go along for a dozen years on end, giving most of their energies and thought to meeting a modest budget, never in history more than $100,000 in any one year, then have a barrage of decisions thrown at them of a dimension overpowering enough to stagger them, something begins to happen! But the men rose to the challenge in one called meeting after another.

A vote was finally taken that I should go to Albuquerque at the convenience of the Shambaughs, at which time there would hopefully be a meeting of minds if indeed we were to proceed. Alice and I invited ourselves to Albuquerque and they graciously accepted.

Flamboyant, dramatic, dynamic, sometimes inscrutable, always intense—what Gilbert's body lacked in vitality seemed to have been compensated by a demanding drive. Impatient, always a "pusher," I was never grilled so long and so astutely by anyone before or since about George Fox College. For several hours into the night and again the next morning, we ranged in animated discussion from questions about the connection with the church, to the academic plans for the future, the calibre of the Board of Trustees, student life, support from the city of Newberg. His questions were piercing and it took every bit of prayerful ingenuity I could muster to come forward with satisfactory answers.

He had given a great deal of thought to the question of why some colleges have grown and prospered, while others have languished and died. Of course, incipient in the generic question was the specific situation of Pacific and George Fox—admitting that George Fox may not have been strong, and an infusion of ready funds could make a dramatic change for the better. And while money in itself cannot guarantee excellence and future greatness, given a strong board and administration, and a keen faculty with ability, imagination, and willingness to innovate, adequate funds could make their dreams come true.

This line of reasoning brought on a series of questions about our future plans. Did I know where I was going? What about long-range plans? What about the future size? Major fields? New properties? Employment for students? How glad I was that the board had adopted a long-range plan! I was able to respond citing minuted action. We had united and the general direction was charted. We had thought through many of his queries. We knew the way we hoped to go—we needed the wherewithal!

Finally, he closed the interview with the words: "You both had better get going back to Oregon. If you stay another day, it may cost me an additional $100,000." It was agreed that formal papers were to be drawn up in their presence at the next meeting of the board in December. This, on August 25.

When I returned to my office I was immediately notified to return a phone call to Albuquerque. It was Gilbert again, impatient and raring to go. Could the board meet immediately? Would better preliminary plans be ready in a short time? Would I arrange a meeting for him and Newberg bankers and business leaders? Yes,

yes, and yes. So it was that he and Olive attended a called meeting of the George Fox Board of Trustees on September 25, 1960.

The previous Sunday, September 23, was Fall Convocation with the college church (Newberg Friends) packed to the rafters, after which pictures of honor students were taken, followed by a reception held at our home. When we arrived at church for the evening service, we were surprised to note that the Shambaughs were not in attendance. We returned home about 10 p.m. I answered the telephone and heard Gilbert on the other end, "Milo, you can have my money!" What we did not realize was that he had attended the Christian Endeavor hour where he was happy to see more than a hundred college students enthusiastically singing rousing choruses, engaging in earnest impromptu prayers, and a number giving thrilling accounts of answers to prayer and evidence of divine action in providing for their return or coming to college. He was so overcome that he asked to be taken home and so we had missed him. I recalled he had been especially critical of youth, but the George Fox collegians, unaware of the biases of the crippled gentleman who sat in the rear of the church, had accomplished for their college what no amount of formal statements or marketing appeals would ever do.

Most of the trustees attended the meeting. When Mr. Shambaugh made his statement of interest, I noticed tears coursing down the face of Dr. John Brougher who through the years had given so generously when the going was rough and it had appeared to him, as well as many others, that support was tantamount to throwing one's money away. Coinciding with the Shambaugh developments was the generous gift of property by Mr. and Mrs. Isaac Smith, long-time patrons of the college. The $25,000 gift by annuity equaled any previous gift to Pacific or George Fox.

The culmination of these sagas up to the actual signing of papers opened up to me as president and to my associates on the board a new door behind which lay a treasure of excitement that none of us had imagined before. Years of preparation went into this fulfillment. Every facet of our constituency sparkled with happiness. The student body burst into applause when I brought the news at dinner in the dining hall at which time the Shambaughs were present. At first the students did not grasp the connection, not knowing them personally, but when the realization dawned, they rose in a standing ovation. People in the churches could not accept all the wonder of it, and I had the happy duty of recounting and explaining wherever I went.

I think that my personal reaction was one of confirmation, that the ideas I was formulating about fund raising must be sound. As I began to rub shoulders with men "in the know," gleaning information from lectures and books, I had a completely new realization of possibilities with which to solicit support for the college.

Most of this valuable input came through the Council for the Advancement of Small Colleges (CASC). Much of the subject matter, other than the process of accreditation concerned itself with finance. Leaders who associated with us were involved in finance, fund-raising, development, foundations, or public relations. Leaders of corporations, officers of the Council for Financial Aid to Education, the American Fund-Raising Council, and the Independent College Funds of America were represented and shared their knowledge and expertise.

THE NEXT SPRING the CASC office in Washington, D.C., planned a guided, educational fund-raising trip into New York City. Since we were to invite our staff people, Denver Headrick and I went together. This was his first trip to the east coast and I had never seen the city from the air so I was as excited as Denver. Our program was to call on assigned executives two by two, report back for evening debriefing, then return for new appointments the next day. Everything was thrilling and novel: the great hotels, eating out, the fabulous office suites, the timing of appointments, even the New York phones. I don't recollect all of my appointments, but my interviews at Union Carbide, National Dairy Products, and Olin-Matheson come to mind. Denver had an exciting time—he was on the team that visited U.S. Steel. All in all, those days in New York were worth a million dollars, and more! These openings and the growing sense of confidence have been of inestimable value to all of our endeavors since. We shared our experience with each other, and again with the trustees. The cumulative effect continues.

I write these lines while I am basking in the light of a very gracious letter which arrived in today's post from Maurice Chandler. In it he tells of his recent visit with Ray Kooi, of the Ford Motor Company Fund, in his office in Dearborn, Michigan. Ray had sent along his personal greetings which takes my mind back to my first visit with him. We needed to fund an impending workshop on college management to be held under the leadership of CASC on the campus of Michigan State University. We received the grant, making Ford the sponsor of the event; Mr. Kooi himself attended and made a significant personal contribution.

I had also asked for favorable consideration for George Fox College. The entire visit, with all of its ramifications, is still vivid in my memory, reminding me of this and other adventures through the years. Although some of the details are embarrassing to me personally, I think now, at long last, they can be entered upon the record.

I refer to the eastern trip I took with Allen Hadley. Returning from Maine, Boston, and New York City, we separated — he coming directly back home to Portland, and I going to Detroit to have the interview with Kooi. I had my United Airlines ticket on through to Portland with a stopover in Detroit, and thinking I should need but little money, I had reduced my cash for sightseeing down to a five dollar bill. After all, I was to be in Portland late that evening with the family car to meet me.

I left Newark in the morning looking toward an afternoon meeting in Dearborn, and although I should have known better, somehow it had not gotten through to me that Willow Run Airport is way out in Ypsilanti, thirty miles away! I checked on the most economical transportation and was shocked to find it cost nearly five dollars via the interurban Greyhound bus. Double checking, I bought a ticket to an intermediate junction for $3.95 and walked the last three or four miles to the American Road offices, arriving hot and hurried without much time to spare. We had our interview and Ray asked what time my plane left for the west, to which I replied, "Seven-thirty this evening."

So he went ahead, "With all of that time on our hands, why don't we go through the Dearborn Museum?" We closed up his office about 3 p.m. and went on over to the museum. Of course, he took me in as his guest, and I don't know when I have spent a more enjoyable, educational, and profitable two hours. He was an informed and delightful guide, choosing (it seemed to me) the very best to observe in our limited time. But in the back of my mind all the while was the nagging, worrying question, "How am I to get the thirty miles to the airport?"

We returned in good spirits to the main offices and made a special tour where a new series of Thunderbirds were stored under wraps. By that time it was at least five-thirty. Finally, he said, "How are you getting to Willow Run?"

That was a hard one! It might not be in the best interests of higher education and George Fox College in particular if he were to know that I was down to $1.05! In a wink I responded, "Oh, I came in on the Greyhound." He proceeded to insist, "That's a long, tiring trip, what with the evening traffic and all; let me call my chauffeur. He can get you there in half the time." With that he summoned a liveried driver, and I was whisked away to the airport in a black Thunderbird! You can add your own moral. There is a saying among college presidents, "No one will give money if he knows your college needs it."

SOME INCIDENTAL OBSERVATIONS come to mind with clarity for our own situation. In Augusta, Maine, at a CASC conference, Allen Hadley and I heard Paul Davis, a leading counselor in the field. He stated that pride was what prompted people to give. It was the hope of lasting fame, one's name high on a list of donors, recognition among one's peers—family, alumni, public-spirited citizens. He believed this was true even among humble church stewards.

The concept was new and shocking to me. Growing up as I had where pastoral salaries were small and some Quakers did not donate to the "hireling ministry," and where the left hand is not to know the action of the right, to sublimate the emotions and mix them with pride was something I had to get used to. Could we take pride in the work of the Lord's kingdom? Could a higher steward-ship be achieved from our constituency? Were there deeper levels of support which could be tapped if sophisticated techniques were employed? These were the questions which I debated and prayed over night and day; eventually I saw their rightness and the value of using them. My conversations with Gilbert Shambaugh depended heavily on what I had learned from Davis. After our successes in cooperation with the Shambaughs, I wired Davis and received a complimentary reply.

In like manner, I learned much from Jerry Burns of the Independent College Funds of America. Denver Headrick and I were participants in a workshop led by him at Portland State College, and in answer to the question I put to him, "Which college is likely to get the money?" his answer was promptly and unhesi-tatingly, "the one with the best prepared application." Here again, I was not ready to accept the answer. After years of being turned down, I had gotten to the place where I was ready to admit that the "big ones get the big money." But two sets of circumstances proved to me the correctness of Burns' answer. The first was a pro-posal presented to the Louis H. and Maud Hill Family Foundation. I worked on the application for weeks. I gave it my best effort, even to "hiding out" at our beach cabin for some days. All of this paid off in a three-year grant totaling $145,000.

The second incident is in two parts—the first negative and dis-appointing, and the other highly successful. In the Higher Education Act of 1965, there was a classification for Developing Colleges, and after receiving advice both in Portland and San Francisco, I prepared an application and sent it off. It was turned down. Later the same year we were encouraged to resubmit. I turned the assignment over to Dr. Lansing Bulgin, Chancellor of the Association of Christian Colleges of Oregon. He worked over his data painstakingly for weeks. He conducted work sessions involving the leaders of the three schools. He phoned Washington, D. C., securing exact directions on procedure. He eventually came up with a masterful presentation which won for us the tidy grant of $125,000 with the anticipation of sustained and successive grants over the next five years. As a sequel, his proposal was chosen by Health, Education, and Welfare for its excellence and we were allowed a bonus grant of $15,000 to assist consortia to improve their future applications.

AT THIS JUNCTURE in the narrative it may be well to pay tribute to faithful supporters who have given over the years. It is too easy to lionize more recent, larger donors, but later victories depended heavily on the loyalty of earlier friends. Within the time limit of this history, I think primarily of trustees who gave of their time and concern and earthly store.

Frank Colcord created the first athletic scholarship. Dr. John Brougher, as a result of the promptings of Dr. Gervais Carey, gave generously to the science hall which now bears his name. I soon learned that the Broughers were very imaginative and deeply concerned people. They gave to many needy causes, specifically for pre-nursing and later premedical scholarships (one of their endowment trusts has sustained this in perpetuity); for the general fund in time of crisis; to add a new wing onto the science hall; for new science equipment; for special projects in the college museum; for new properties for housing and future expansion. He was constantly putting in a good word to people who were well placed and afterward writing letters of appreciation to them.

I think of the Everett and Bertha Heacock family. They established the first underwritten and sustaining scholarship program in our history. In May, 1935, I preached on the subject of managed stewardship at the First Friends Church in Portland where the family had attended for many years. I questioned the short-sighted community living of the early church where the capital assets of the group were quickly exhausted. I advanced the idea of making investments early in life so that one's resources for stewardship and giving could be greater in later years. I went home with them for dinner. During the course of after-dinner conversation in his den, we worked out a plan for funds for quarterly meeting scholarships in increasing increments as the amount of tuition increased. Nor was this generous contribution to be the last. His sons-in-law, Wilbert Eichenberger and Eldon Helm, followed along in the enlightened family tradition. Especially with Wilbert's active involvement on the Board of Trustees, the family resources kept pace with many projects of the college year by year. They supported at a top level all of the drives, including one for a great share of the furnishings in Heacock Commons itself. Wilbert had a way of quietly contributing to needed but unheralded projects, most of which he, the business office, and I were the only ones in the know.

Dr. Homer Hester was one to always come through when we most needed it. Being on the investment committee and the finance committee, he was on the inside track of many programs to improve finances. He would slip in $500 or $1,000 to give a new project a good start, or be responsible for the last amount to put it over the top. I am sure that he must have often put in a good word to our bankers. He signed papers at the right times.

As the Board of Trustees gained new members, I think especially of Phil Martin from Whittier, California. A self-made inventor and engineer, his special interest was science. At the time he joined the group, we were going through the throes of low salaries, competition for our talent, and the difficulty of getting and keeping young scholars who were working toward graduate programs.

I recall a luncheon in southern California with Dr. Eugene Coffin. Out of the animated discussion that day, Phil offered to assist by giving a bonus summer salary to several professors; from

$600 to $1200 was added to the salaries of our professors so that they could support themselves in summer study. This was especially critical among professors in the science fields, owing to keen competition from industry, government, and larger universities. Thus, for a number of years one eager professor after another enjoyed the stimulus and security that the bonus brought. Some took much-needed refresher courses, some worked on their doctorates, others were released to do research. All of us—the college, the professors, their disciplines, the students, and I dare say Phil Martin himself—profited greatly. I can think of no finer service to this important segment of the enterprise.

I TRUST THAT THESE illustrations will suffice, although I hope that not highlighting every donor and their projects will not be taken amiss. These are the building blocks for later financial success and stability. For example, Dr. Shambaugh was very insistent that I explain to him about these men, their calibre, and their commitment. Without their willingness over the years to have "put it there," later great friends of the cause would never have materialized. In talking to foundation and corporation executives, one of the first questions often asked was "What is the competition doing?" Willingness to be first in an untried cause is a noble trait indeed.

Looking at it another way, this type of gift is called "seed money." Gilbert Shambaugh, after having been convinced of the rightness of the George Fox cause, the probability of a solid future, and the faithfulness of the trustees at the time, was willing to step forward. He became part of a chain reaction that did not stop with him. Almost immediately he had a meeting with Sidney Collier, vice president and superintendent of the Spaulding Pulp and Paper Company, asking for Sid's good will and good work obtaining corporate support for the college. He also wrote M. Lowell Edwards, telling Lowell of his interest and pleasure in supporting the college. The results of these two important contacts cannot be overstated.

*F*OR FEAR THAT anyone may think we experienced only success, it is my painful duty to admit that some of the big ones got away—a college president hates to admit these failures as much as does an ardent fisherman. Actually, the percentage of dramatic, favorable response is exceedingly small compared with larger universities. A primary principle of fund raising is simply to maintain and add to a list of friends. If a small college has only 5,000 on its mailing list, and in that list only several hundred alumni, potential for investors is very small indeed. If, instead, a large university lists 100,000, 200,000 or more among its constituency, the likelihood of favorable response is that much greater. Some universities benefit from world-wide reputations, and there are instances of very large donations from unknown patrons who were never cultivated. But we have never undergone such an astonishing experience!

I remember when our mailing list exceeded 3,500 by only a few names. We continued to meet corporate executives and prospective donors within a fifty-mile radius who had never heard of George Fox College. In such situations, my esteemed associate, Denver Headrick, was of inestimable assistance. He was simply priceless as a courteous, painstaking, friend-maker because for every one hundred interviews, there were one hundred more friends, several dozen more who would receive our literature, one or two more who could be depended upon to invest. We went on adding to our donor base; traveling to new states and cities; making the rounds to foundations in New York, Chicago, San Francisco, Los Angeles; appearing before clubs and churches and alumni groups in Washington, D. C., or Denver or Wichita or Phoenix or Spokane.

I have made a rule never to let a day go by without asking for money! The request may take the form of a letter or a telephone call or some more general appeal, but as often as not, I meet over coffee, take a friend out to lunch, or discuss things off in a corner at a reception. As an administrative procedure, Denver and I, and more recently Maurice Chandler, employ a method we call "spiraling" where we are always on the lookout for possible new investors as some fields become less fruitful, or individuals cease to be interested or are unable to respond favorably.

I HAVE ALREADY MENTIONED how some colleges are fortunate enough to be named by hitherto unknown donors. We had one experience which, although not a very large gift, was something we would like to have repeated. In the summer of 1956 my office received a letter in penciled longhand, addressed simply, "President, " from a lady in Bremerton, Washington. She was the sister of a deceased Mr. John Anderson, whose will was now in court and named George Fox College as beneficiary of $12,000. In due course, we received the sum, although in ways which were to be stranger than fiction.

I called her on the phone, suspecting that it was a hoax — that there was no such name or listing — but I heard a cheery voice which confirmed the letter. We made a search of our alumni files to ascertain if he had ever attended. We conferred with older professors, and especially with Dr. Pennington, none of whom had ever heard of said John Anderson. To complicate the mystery, the sister and her husband admitted that he was a bachelor recluse; as far as they knew he had never mentioned George Fox (in fact, neither of them had even heard of the college) but in his effects was an envelope and a sheet of George Fox stationery. Later, we contacted alumni who had at one time lived in Bremerton, but none had ever heard of the old gentleman.

At the end of the first six months of probate, I made the trip to Bremerton to confer with the attorney in charge of the settlement. Everything was in order, George Fox College was the first named beneficiary, and there were sufficient assets to cover all of the claims. The others named were a Jewish charity and a playground project. But there was one detail which needed to be cleared. The assets were not all liquid, being tied up in real estate both in Seattle and California. There was an income property in Ballard appraised at $12,000 which the judge had assigned to the college. The advantage was that by assigning now, we could have the lease income pending a sale which might take some time. I asked if there were responsible tenants, the amount of the rent, and about our accepting or rejecting the plan. To which she answered, "There are very good renters. In fact, they have occupied the premises for several years and they wish to continue, if possible. The rental income is $350 per month, one half coming from a tavern and the other from a rescue mission."

To show the humor of the case, we had just completed a victorious election campaign to "keep Newberg dry." I had been the chair of the temperance forces under which Dr. Homer Hester had been elected mayor on the dry ticket and other trustees and college people had been active in the campaign. Now, to top it all off, the college owned a tavern in Seattle, and would be receiving money from its rental for the general operation! I refused to sign the full release on the grounds that we were not a Washington corporation (which was the one option available) but allowed the checks to come through from the court until after three or four months a Seattle broker bought up our paper. A wet $12,000 check helped us through a dry summer.

A SUBSTANTIAL DONOR of long standing was Amos Stuart, founder of the Carnation Company, and his successors. The Stuarts, unknown to many westerners, were North Carolina Quakers, and Amos had served on the board of Guilford College in Greensboro at one time. The story of his company and its movement to Wisconsin, then to Seattle, and finally to Los Angeles, and its listing among the one hundred greatest corporations, is not for this book. The sustained interest in George Fox College is.

Now, I do not know the details of all of the interviews between Amos, then Elbridge (his son), and Levi Pennington. However, suffice it to say they must have been altogether satisfactory, for when Levi was forced to retire in 1939 and a drive was launched to create an endowment for the president emeritus, the Stuarts came forward with $25,000 in Carnation stock. The basic endowment was established, and it grew under the wise control of our investment committee. Thus, Levi Pennington received adequate compensation for his old age.

Of course, a person must start at the beginning, working from the known to the unknown. The first executive of any firm I was to call upon in Los Angeles in regards to the endowment was Mr. Ruddick, vice president of the Carnation Company and president of the Foundation. In preparation for my visit, I had gone back over old trustee business and conferred with the investment committee, finding that the limitations on the use of the income from the original $25,000 were relaxed at the end of twenty-five years. Twenty-five years were up as of June, 1964.

This discovery made renewed correspondence and a Los Angeles visit a reasonable development, out of which Mr. Ruddick and I came up with a proposal for work grants which would be awarded to student assistants. These assistants were to be superior, ambitious students, chosen by their major professors, who would benefit from the experience of working with them. For example, a senior in English might receive a grant of $150 per annum to grade freshman composition papers and monitor tests. Perhaps an outstanding student would be an assistant for a physics professor and set up equipment for demonstrations for $200 per year. To put this in perspective, the financial assistance to the student was substantial when gross annual tuition was $350. Student assistants released professors to engage in more meaningful tasks, and at the same time created opportunities for these students to gain valuable experience.

The plan, as then conceived and later adopted and expanded, continues to be one of the most imaginative we have implemented. An element of the program's success in the eyes of Mr. Ruddick, was the feedback we provided. Year after year, biographies of the assistants, their assignments, and an evaluation of their experiences were prepared and submitted just prior to the meeting of the

Carnation and Stuart boards. Mr. Ruddick was kind enough to tell me that our reporting was the best of any recipient among all of their world-wide benefactions.

ENVER HEADRICK'S first "scoop" came in a normal, and yet round-about way. He had been on the staff but a few months when a number of us had the privilege of attending the Evangelical Friends Church conference in Denver, Colorado. Denver made up a carload to cut expenses for the college. While at the conference two of the young women in his party prevailed upon him to go "the long way home" across Nevada to San Francisco, promising to pay the added cost. After considering it, we agreed, especially as he had not done any fund raising before in that area.

While my party and I drove directly back to Oregon, Denver, with very little preparation or background, hit the great city by the Golden Gate. Its business community was none too hospitable, to say the least, in mid-summer; in fact, many executives and foundation secretaries were on vacation. But he did get into the main offices of Crown-Zellerbach.

Charles A. Stine met him and they hit it off from the very beginning. Our list of reasons for asking for support was not a very long one at the time, but we could claim: proximity in Oregon to the major paper mill at West Linn; one of Crown-Zellerbach's log dumps at Dundee some two miles from Newberg; and a number of former students who had worked their way through college at the great mill at Camas. It was not a very big "bag of tricks."

But Denver must have made a good impression on Mr. Stine, for (as we were to discover) some wheels started rolling. Through the college grapevine we heard that a Crown-Zellerbach representative from West Linn had been commissioned to inquire about the little college in Newberg. He went to the good people at Lewis and Clark, and they gave us a clean bill of health. Then, unannounced, a young man by the name of Zellerbach came out to view the campus. Only by chance I saw this strange young fellow wandering about the place taking pictures. A few months later, we received a check for $1,000, an amount we continued to receive every spring. With it we were asked to set up a scholarship for a deserving student—$600 to go to the student and $400 matching to the college itself. Thus, we had our first matching scholarship. Also, Crown Zellerbach wanted things done right. Could there be some type of public recognition at which time an engraved certificate could be presented? This request gave us the major impetus to establish and maintain the Fall Convocation when scholarships and honors are distributed publicly and appreciation is expressed to the donors.

We made it a rule to visit Mr. Stine or one of the other executives at their international office at least once a year. These meetings proved to be as rewarding as any we have had. Without a doubt, we are convinced that what Crown-Zellerbach gave us as "seed money" was of far greater value than the $1,000 per year! We used it with great effectiveness in all of our accreditation documents, and alluded to it in every case with prospective donors. Grants from the C. S. Johnston Foundation and Southern Pacific were most assuredly a direct result, and at least an open ear was gained in the northwest where so many of our contacts were with timber, lumber, paper, plywood, and related industries. Its significance has not been lost on the Calder interests and more recently, friends at Publishers Paper Company.

THE CALDER STORY is a tale throbbing with emotion and an interplay of personal interest at many levels. It begins with two old gentlemen living in different suites at the Astor Towers on Park Avenue in New York City. One was an elderly Scottish immigrant whose saga parallels the American story. He had gotten into oil many years ago and built the first chain of gasoline pumping stations in the country, later selling out to Standard Oil of New Jersey. One thing led to another, but it was apparent that moneymaking was his forte. He developed many companies, but in later years he concentrated on paper products. His investments came to be grouped in a hidden foundation which owned his corporations—exactly the opposite of more recent business practice. His name was Louis Calder. The Louis Calder Foundation owned the Perkins-Goodwin Corporation of 1 Rockefeller Plaza, New York City.

The other old gentleman was Herbert Hoover, thirty-first president of the United States, who had graduated from Friends Pacific Academy at Newberg, Oregon, in 1891. They often spent long evenings together, and so it was that the name "Newberg" came into the conversation one night. Calder mentioned that one of his companies had bought a paper mill there, and Hoover described his boyhood years. So much for one strand of the story.

Another thread was the inconsequential choice of a career paper man to take over the reins of the small, struggling mill in Newberg. His name was Sidney Collier from Washington who came originally from the paper industry in western Canada. He took over the mill with ambitions to improve it, to say the least. An orphan mill, it boasted no steady market and its equipment was obsolete. Sid set about to find ways to raise the necessary capital to modernize. Several major corporations looked into the possibility of investing in the mill, only to turn them down. Out of the blue, the Perkins-Goodwin Corporation of New York City bought the controlling interest and things began to happen. I cannot recall the exact chronology, but an addition doubled or tripled the mill's capacity. The entire operation was made shipshape resulting in up-to-date efficiency and opening more full time jobs.

Sid had always taken an interest in public and school affairs and now he and Frank Colcord were both serving on the local hospital board. Sid had made significant and leading inquiries into the remodeling and expanding needs of the hospital. Frank took me aside and said, "Milo, I think there must be a foundation in the picture somewhere. Why don't you try to get some money for the college?" Denver and I made a search in the Russell Sage book of foundations where we found a listing of the Louis Calder Foundation incorporated in the state of New York. The assets were worth $26,000,000. Frank was correct!

Without showing my hand, I went to Sid, gained an interview in his office, took a tour of the mill with its new look, and brought up our needs for the science department. The science hall needed more equipment for which Hector Munn had presented me a list. Sid did not resent my impertinence; I did not tell him I knew of any foundation. But in a few weeks he informed me that he could extend some hope for my request. Then he called and said he had received a message from New York promising $5,000. Next (and this was to be the way that Sid operated) he suggested that the gift be made at a supper to be served at the local Bowman's Cafe with him picking up the tab. How many college personnel did I wish to be present?

It proved to be a beautiful occasion. Sid presided as master of ceremonies. At the end of the evening, he grouped a number of us in a semicircle around him in front of the cameras—Ivan Adams of the board, Dr. Hester as mayor, Mel Dunston for the Chamber, Hector Munn for the science faculty, and myself—when all at once I heard the announcement that the Calder Foundation would be giving $25,000! Honestly, there had been a message they would be giving $5,000. It was at least that! We had our first break with Calder.

THE ENSUING five years were dramatic for all of us. With two sizable checks, the Calder interests made possible the remodel and addition to the science hall. At one time another $25,000 was advanced to provide fringe benefits for the faculty. With it, the Teachers Insurance and Annuity Association-College Retirement Equities Fund (TIAA-CREF) retirement program was put into effect, and the entire faculty received a Christmas bonus.

As far as benefits to the faculty are concerned, nothing better than the TIAA has ever come their way. It and other programs have proved providential to thousands for the last three or more generations. Heavily endowed by Carnegie, it offers generous benefits in retirement, plus various peripheral programs in investments, hospital and medical coverage, and more. The first year Calder paid not only the college's 5 percent, but the participating faculty's as well. In the intervening years, the advantages have become clear to one and all, but most of all to those who, in their terminal illnesses have depended heavily on the largesse of its ample provision.

The key to qualifying for funds from the Louis Calder Foundation was found to be in a limiting provision in the charter of the Foundation: all grants were to be made in educational or cultural interests only in geographical areas of the company operations. Thus, to put it plainly, the purchase of the Newberg mill by the Perkins-Goodwin Corporation and George Fox College being located in Newberg, were the two important qualifications for receiving grants. If they had bought a mill in Portland or Salem, we should not have qualified. Their nearest mill heretofore was located in Wisconsin. None of them had ever heard of George Fox College. From any angle, the train of circumstances added up to a breathtaking providence. There were no legal obstacles to hinder; no impossible hurdles. Of course, foundations do not give money without cause. It was up to us to present a case, or a number of cases, to merit the continued support of the leadership in New York City.

When I went to see Reinhold Dreher in the Foundation offices in April, 1964, I was given to understand that any future grants would be for student aid. Then, Mr. Calder passed away. I was assured by Sid Collier that his death would not greatly change the nature or extent of the Foundation's interest.

On the 30th of July, 1964, I received a letter from Mr. Dreher, in the name of the trustees of the Foundation, stating that a decision had been reached to build a memorial to Mr. Calder on the George Fox campus. Could I come forward with a proposition or set of plans and estimates? I got New York on the phone within the hour to thank him and find out a little more of his thinking. True, they needed ideas; no exact direction had been given. It was up to us to present something acceptable both in nature and cost to him and his associates. I was so excited I could have jumped over a roof!

It goes without saying that we held many meetings in the next several days, concluding with a called meeting of the trustees. Our initial proposal for a new auditorium to be used for a chapel and fine arts center was rejected because of Mr. Calder's lack of interest in the arts. He had been a rough-hewn man caring not at all for symphonies or art shows.

So we started over. Our second proposal, for a new science hall was greeted and accepted with enthusiasm. Chemistry and botany were very easily defended as undergraduate studies in forestry and paper-making. Also, we had a genuine need due to the dramatic growth of the college as a whole and science in particular, requiring more room and more sophisticated equipment. Mathematics and physics were to stay in Brougher Hall. Chemistry and biology were to move, along with two other general fields, home economics and foreign language. Altogether, the new complex would increase available teaching space significantly.

The faculty that would be involved in the actual use of the building worked diligently throughout the summer with Donald Lindgren, our architect. In almost no time it seemed, with his office cooperating full time, Don created a startling, imaginative design for Calder Center [now Lemmons Center] composed of three hexagons—designed in the shape of a water molecule. A lecture hall and faculty offices were to be housed in the center core with classrooms like cuts of a pie ringing the outside of the building. Internal halls were to be reduced to a minimum—students could enter the laboratories from an ample, covered porch. Everyone was thrilled with the possibilities. Armed with the drawings, I prepared to fly to New York City.

All of the Calder leadership was present for the meeting— Louis, Jr., who at the age of forty-four had taken over after his father's death, Reinhold Dreher, and John Foxgrover. Foxgrover launched into a strong recital of Sid Collier's good assets, claiming that we would never have gotten a cent were it not for him. Dreher, meanwhile, brought up personal reactions to the George

Fox situation, stating that his first wish years before had been to allow only $10,000 for sidewalks! I was pretty nervous. We assumed something tangible was forthcoming and the general idea of a science hall had been approved, but the crucial moment arrives when one mentions the exact estimated cost. I knew I had their tacit approval from the looks on their faces. They were very pleased, indeed, with the sketches. They liked everything they saw and all that I tried to explain. They were especially intrigued with the hexagon shape which allowed for so great a number of students to be handled in the floor space. Coupled with the general shape, they liked the idea of a minimum use of hallways which would reduce requirements for heat and light and maintenance. We talked for an hour or more before Mr. Dreher asked the fateful money question. I had to answer, "We will require at least $300,000," which was the figure given to me by Don Lindgren. I saw the men look at each other. Then Mr. Dreher spoke for the three: "We will give you $300,000. It will have to come over a period of months, but I shall put in writing a letter of intent."

We had won! What I did not know until much later was that prior to my coming, the Calder board had put a ceiling on their proposed gift at $200,000. But, seeing the very clever plans, they had increased it by common consent by another $100,000. The argument over whether or not a good architect pays for himself has its answer as far as our experience is concerned. And we take off our hats to the Calder trustees, who, although they possessed the resources, could have held to their original amount, but who had the wisdom and generosity to make an adequate memorial.

Eventually, the Los Angeles Times-Mirror, through its subsidiary Publishers Paper Company, bought out the interests of the Louis Calder Foundation in Newberg. Sid Collier went his way, but was granted an honorary doctorate from my hand.

AS FAR BACK AS 1957, I had heard about the activities of the Louis H. and Maud Hill Family Foundation. It had given the first sustaining grant to the Oregon Colleges Foundation. Its northwest representative, David Mason, was a courtly gentle-man, one-time president of the Oregon Historical Society. The Foundation put out an annual report revealing that it was founded on timber wealth, that it gave to historical and cultural enterprises of the northwest — meaning anywhere from Minnesota to Puget Sound. Its interest included theaters and symphonies and educational television, mostly in the Minneapolis-Saint Paul area, but as far afield as western South Dakota. Armed with this background, Denver and I had several interviews with Mr. Mason, not without some encouragement, and learned that there could be interest in summer theater of a historical nature. The key to Hill's support, we were told, would be found in outstanding leadership.

There followed months of work to build a case for the summer theater, but in the end the plans broke down and nothing came together. Then at a meeting in February, 1964, Denver learned that Mr. Mason hoped to lay hands on an Oregon project worthy of the support of Hill — the other states to the east had had their share of late. Denver brought up the idea of inter-institutional cooperation, a kind of pooling of resources by George Fox and others. By this time, the possibility was already being investigated with Cascade and Warner Pacific colleges, but at that time there were no commitments, no legal action, no operating procedures, no mandate from any board. But then Mr. Mason reacted: "Why don't we follow up on these ideas? I think I could champion such a program as you have suggested." So before the interview was concluded, it had been agreed that the three of us — Mr. Mason, Denver, and I — were to have a subsequent meeting after some thought had been given by all concerned. Denver was ecstatic! He had broken through at last.

Some five months later the three of us met over lunch at the Pine Room at Meier and Frank. Mr. Mason gave us every encouragement to proceed. Thereafter, working with the two other presidents, Dr. Lewis Gough and Thomas Leupp, we came to sufficient meeting of minds for me to gather the necessary data. Our executive committee was to give sufficient backing. I took three days off at our beach cabin and hammered out a proposal. To date, it was the most ambitious proposal of its kind in my career, adding up to some $175,000 over a three-year period. Refining it in conference, my secretary prepared it and I submitted it to Mr. Mason.

As was his method, he acknowledged it promptly, congratulating me on its features. Our proposal was referred to Dr. A. A. Heckman of St. Paul, Minnesota, who was to come to Portland in October and the presidents of the three colleges could anticipate a working session with him. All of which came to be. His final word after our meeting was that he too could support the proposal in its revised form. Later, in April, 1965, the full board approved its first grant to the Associated Christian Colleges of Oregon in the sum of $144,700 to be distributed over a three year period. This first grant supported the joint enterprise up to June 30, 1967. On December 12, 1967, a second major allotment of $145,000 came through to fund the program until June 30, 1971. Thus, building on study and adapting to the wishes of a great foundation, we were fortunate indeed, to receive a series of grants totaling almost $300,000.

OUR NEXT SAGA is one of a family of early Northwest Quakers whose lives, fortunes, and interests had been closely tied with the college from its inception. The first of the clan to come West were Jesse and Mary Edwards, both Friends ministers from Indiana. (Jesse was a brother of my great-grandmother.) They made their way in the early 1880s to San Francisco via Union and Central Pacific railroad; then up the coast to Portland; via river boats up the Willamette River and Yamhill River to Dayton; and last by hired rig to what is now Newberg. Their farm occupied the portion of Newberg bounded by First Street and South College, and from there south and west to the river. In addition to farming, Jesse built a brick-making business.

He gave brick to build the Friends Meeting House (now Newberg Friends Church) which still stands as a monument to the vision and stewardship of these pioneers. His sons attended

Pacific Academy and College. Clarence came to be one-half of the first graduating class of 1892. The other half was Amos Stanbrough, and it was claimed by these classmates that in all their years of either class meetings or class reunions, they always had a one hundred percent attendance! After graduation, Clarence worked in the electric power industry while Amos went into education. The other Edwards son, Oren K., or "O.K." as he was nicknamed, followed his father in the family business which later became the famous Willamina Clay Products Company.

The Willamina yards came to produce some of the finest brick in the country, so out of loyalty and yet with an eye to value, the college board specified it for Wood-Mar Hall in 1911-12, and much later to face Brougher, the science hall, in 1947. Oren carried on the business until his death in 1960. The last time I saw him alive was at Herbert Hoover's eighty-first birthday party. When I preached his funeral some months later, I first met Gerald, his son, who was to take over as president of the business. He was living in Willamina at the time, but soon moved to Tigard, and it came to be that we were to have a great deal of contact over the years as we continued to buy larger and larger orders of brick for our new buildings. He had attended Stanford and Harvard universities, never having come to Pacific. His revived interest in the college may be attested by his willingness to discount 10 percent and later 15 percent on all our orders for brick. His wife became terminally ill and passed away, and he asked me to conduct the service for him and his family.

Afterward, he and I became very good friends indeed. He would take me out to breakfast, I accompanied him on business trips, Alice and I would have him in for a meal. Then cupid, in the form of a lovely, refined Christian woman came into the picture—Elizabeth Aebischer by name. They met formally at the 1963 Commencement dinner where she was a hostess and he a guest. Elizabeth, as an alumna, had proved her loyalty to her alma mater in many ways as president of the alumni association, and at the time she met Gerald she was working on staff as an admissions officer. They were married at the Chapel of the Hills and nothing could have been better for both of them. He renewed his vows to God and became very active in Newberg Friends Church. Their acts of stewardship and love for the college cause went on from one need to the next. Later she was elected to the Board of Trustees.

Jesse Edwards' other son, Clarence, started the Newberg Electric Company in his own woodshed, building it up to become the Yamhill Electric Company which eventually became a division of Portland General Electric Company. He later was involved in management at the Mountain States Power Company which was absorbed into Pacific Power and Light. He served on the college board for many years. His sons, Lowell and Lloyd, both attended Pacific College. Lowell stayed for two years, studying mathematics under Oliver Weesner and attending the classes of Professor Shambaugh, but eventually took his degree in engineering at Oregon Agricultural College (now Oregon State University). On both sides of the house, whether tracing it from Oren to Gerald, or from Clarence to Lowell and Lloyd, very little connection was maintained with Newberg or the college for many intervening years.

My first personal connection with Lowell came through a visit I had with him at his Multnomah laboratory in the summer of 1955, there to solicit money for the Advance. He was cordial and straightforward, but not too responsive. He allowed me to talk and then asked me to return another day, not giving me much encouragement. When I returned, I was to learn that he had discussed my visit with Mrs. Edwards and they had agreed between themselves not to support the college. His response to me went something like this: "I have watched the college over all of these years and it appears that every other school makes progress except Pacific—George Fox. My father served on the board, but became so disaffected that he shifted his loyalties to Willamette, and joined its board. Personally, I don't see any hope for the place. I think, if I may say so, Ross, you are throwing your life away. I am interested in medical research. At the present time I am associated with Dr. Starr here at the University Medical School and we hope to come up with an invention or two. I am now making a donation to the Medical School of $20,000 which very well may not be my last. Whatever we have to give will go that way, and I doubt if there will be any left over. Now you have come here twice. We asked you to come this second time. Mrs. Edwards and I will give you $50 for your trouble. Here is a check. But I suggest that you not come again for a donation to the Newberg college. This is our last gift."

That was to be the end. I did not see him again until after the Christmas season of 1962-63. I did not bother him in any way. Sometime between our Multnomah visit and 1962, he had moved his major operations to Santa Ana, California. He kept a summer residence on the Zigzag River near Mount Hood, but lived during the winters in southern California, building the Edwards Laboratories on Dyer Road. The heart valve, to which he referred in 1955, had been perfected and was now under full production, already making him world renowned. Because of family interests, they made the northern trip at Christmas visiting friends enroute.

And so it was that they stopped off in Newberg to pay their respects to Levi Pennington, whom they greatly admired and respected. Standing on the front porch after their visit, Levi pointed over proudly to the new Pennington Hall, exclaiming, "See what they have done in honor of Rebecca and me!" The Edwards turned to see the gleaming brick and glass dormitory named in honor of the Penningtons. To say they were amazed would be an understatement. True, they had received some "junk" mail now and then from the college, but they never read it. They had no idea that enough progress had been made to allow construction of a building of the proportions of Pennington Hall. It was beautiful and altogether impressive.

Nothing would do but that Levi should show them about. So, even though it was the Christmas holidays and no one but the Cravens were in the dorm, they showed them into the attractive lounge, the private rooms, the provisions for study and recreation, and the fine apartments. Lowell sized things up at a glance. Chairs, yes. A piano, yes. Even potted plants, yes. But no stereo. Before he left, he wrote out a check to the college for $1,000 asking that a good stereo be purchased for the students, the balance to go for classical recordings.

The spell was broken. I had kept faith. He himself had made the first move. We worked together over the next weeks, with me writing and he phoning from wherever he was at the moment, until we secured the finest Zenith stereo system and some $200 worth of excellent records. We worked together with honesty and respect. He knew and I knew that our developments were of such a quality that he could no longer stand by without some financial involvement with his boyhood school.

By the time of the stereo gift, the board had already decided to name the next dormitory "Edwards." The former Edwards Hall, an old house refitted into a boy's dorm, was anything but a fitting memorial to such an illustrious family, but Lowell's renewed interest and gifts in kind from Gerald brought the dream to reality. The Edwards family of today was to be honored as much as the pioneers. Federal financing for a building involves a formula dictating a division of items between solid, built-in, integral portions, and movable furnishings. Government loans do not cover the furniture. Thus, while a college can get financing for the building itself through a government loan, it is forced to look to its own resources for everything from beds to chairs, from draperies to lounge furniture, and from washing machines to waste baskets. The amount, while a small proportion of the total, can be fairly formidable. The Edwards Hall budget had no funding to assist with these needs.

We worked out a budget for the unattached items for Edwards Hall, estimated at between $15,000 and $18,000 at most, and submitted it to Lowell and Margaret. At the same time, since he had mentioned his interest in things scientific, in cooperation with the science faculty, particularly Professor Lawrence Skene and Dr.

John Brewster, I submitted lists of equipment needed in physics, chemistry, and biology. We were very exact and took advantage of sales and discounts, and used these private contributions to apply for matching funds from the National Science Foundation (effectively doubling them). Thus in the next three years, Lowell paid for the purchase of thousands of dollars worth of the most needed, and some of the most sophisticated equipment for all of these sciences. The $25,000 digital computer arrived in 1965. The radio and tower were installed in 1967.

With a man of such calibre, we took action to offer him an honorary doctorate, which was conferred during the Commencement of 1964. The citation read in part:

> As an inventor, engineer, and humanitarian, he serves his present age with distinction. Distinguished son of a pioneer Newberg, Oregon, family, Mr. Edwards attended this college (then named Pacific College) in 1919-20. His father had been in the first graduating class at Pacific College. Mr. M. Lowell Edwards then transferred to Oregon State where he received a degree in electrical engineering in 1924. After three years with General Electric Company in Schenectady, New York, he returned to Portland to enter a partnership in the manufacture of pumps.
>
> In 1927 M. Lowell Edwards moved to Longview, Washington, where he designed and supervised the building of the first hydraulic log barker for the Weyerhaeuser Timber Company. This constituted a significant contribution to the pulp and paper industry. Later, hearing of the difficulties involved in airplane fuel pumps at high altitudes, Mr. Edwards developed successful booster pumps which are used very extensively in military and civilian aircraft.
>
> After World War II, the Edwards family returned to Portland. Here Mr. Edwards became acquainted with a number of medical doctors. Out of these contacts, and his ever-present idea of the importance of engineering to all fields of endeavor including medical science, Mr. Edwards,

in collaboration with a surgeon, Dr. Albert Starr, produced an artificial, ball-type mitral valve to replace damaged natural mitral valves in the human heart. Since the first successful implant of a mitral valve in 1960, thousands of people with damaged hearts now have new hope of an extended, active life.

The name "Edwards" is not new to the George Fox College campus. The newest of our residence halls will honor this pioneer family, whose distinguished scion has not only honored our school by his contributions to society, but has given generously for the furnishings of the new residence hall.

The Psalmist wrote: "Let this be recorded for a generation to come, so that a people yet unborn may praise the Lord: that he looked down from his holy height, from heaven the Lord looked at the earth, to hear the groans of the prisoners, to set free those who were doomed to die; that men may declare in Zion the name of the Lord, and in Jerusalem his praise, when peoples gather together, and kingdoms, to worship the Lord" (Psalm 102:18-22).

In 1965 the board membership was increased from thirty to forty-two so we had vacancies to be filled, and Frank Colcord nominated Lowell. Lowell hesitated and was almost on the verge of declining, but both his wife Margaret and Frank prevailed upon him to accept the appointment, which he did. His election has never been regretted by any concerned.

At the time of his negotiations for the digital computer in late 1965, he confided in Denver and me that he and Margaret had named the college in their wills, and that, because of this future bequest, they might reduce their giving for the immediate future. We launched the first phase of the annuity program, and Denver and I considered the Edwards as likely prospects. In other words, persons known to have put the college in their estates may be the ones who wish to reduce their bequests by prior designation during their life time, thus protecting their interests from punitive taxes.

We arranged ahead for a conference at his Santa Ana offices. But when we broached the subject of annuities, he showed no interest. What he did instead was to outline one of the greatest gifts in the history of the college.

The story begins with his invention of the heart valve and the corporation he founded to put it on the market. He was supplying up to 500 valves monthly to hospitals all over the world and already at least 5,000 lives had been spared. His original investment had multiplied itself many times over, and investors and companies looking toward diversification begin to inquire about taking over. Success makes one's business highly vulnerable to speculation and even eventual takeover. He claimed that hardly a day passed without his being harassed by telephone calls from inquirers. Finally, in order to protect not only his corporation but also his valuable time, he directed all calls to Bache and Company in Los Angeles, listing the sale price so exorbitantly high that he thought none would touch it. It sold in less than ten days! He took stock of the new owner, American Hospital Supply Company of Chicago, and immediately faced the problems of capital gains and other taxes. This was where Denver and I entered the story. Instead of waiting for the bequest to take effect in future years, it would certainly be to his advantage to make a donation now. Would the college be pleased to accept a gift of $140,000 worth of stock in American Hospital?

The announcement hit the headlines of the papers, and was heralded over the radio and television as being the largest amount to have been received by the college in a single day. It proved to be the largest gift for the endowment as well. Our investment committee began to watch the value of American Hospital stock go up and up. At the end of the first year it had increased in value to close to $240,000 and kept on rising. Progress over the months came to be a matter of serious, yet optimistic conjecture by all concerned. Would American Hospital perform in the future as in the immediate past? Might it level off? Would it be affected by the same factors as the total market? How large could we expect the stock to become? Would it be to the advantage of the college to sell all at once, in segments, or exchange for several issues? By June 30, 1968 it had grown to $422,000.

My concern was to work out a satisfactory allocation of the total amount, commensurate with the wishes of Lowell and Margaret, while at the same time ensuring wise use for the future of the college. We reconsidered our aims and strengths, charting what resources would be needed to give a genuine undergirding of them. We kept writing and conferring with Lowell and Margaret. Following is my proposal which, although not final, was accepted by Lowell as a satisfactory guideline:

> The first $200,000 will be reserved as an endowment in pre-medicine. Let us call it the M. Lowell and Margaret Edwards Professorship in Chemistry.

> The second allocation will be for equipment for chemistry in Calder Center. Some $40,000 is included for standard equipment, with added items which may be needed in another two years.

> If there are funds still remaining, we suggest that the third allocation be reserved in the endowment for scholarship aid to premedical students, at a formula to be worked out later.

If we were to realize even a fairly low return from the stock's growth in three years, we could endow our first chair and handle some pressing equipment needs. With a higher rate of return, we could expand into endowed scholarships. The Edwards interest and life aim to assist in the healing arts would find expression in undergraduate chemistry. To emphasize premedical offerings at George Fox would be in full harmony with the basic Christian aims and Quaker tradition. What could be better? By April, 1969, the program should take effect. What added to the delight of the members of the board and Dr. George Moore, Dean of Faculty, was the solid support for basic financial needs. Most of the sizable fund was to remain in endowment, where it would continue growing forever, but all the while restricted to paying faculty salaries. It proved to be a great source of joy to the science faculty. The college, at long last, was to boast an endowed chair!

ANY RESUME of benefactors in recent educational history cannot ignore the role of government. As everyone knows by now, for good or ill (and I trust mainly for good), the federal government is heavily involved in many programs designed to favor the educational establishment. Among our trustees, there has been more honest disagreement and more soul-searching over contractual arrangements with Washington, D. C., than perhaps anything else in our recent history. Not one of the board wanted to accept government funding — myself included. We did not want to embark on an irrevocable course, only to be sorry later. We had genuine fears about compromising our historic position and the separation of church and state. All in all, we have been very cautious. Some of our expressions of displeasure and letters voicing our concern may have significantly influenced the policies under which we operate today. Let us hope so. But we are deeply enmeshed in a number of agreements, accepting hundreds of thousands of dollars for scores of years to come.

The first program, the National Defense Student Loan, began in 1959. This was not a difficult decision to make, and the program is working very well. It has made possible the education of many dozens of needy students.

Next we became involved in loans to finance dormitories, Weesner Village, and Heacock Commons. The main philosophical problem faced in all of these was that a portion of our precious endowment would be tied up to secure the loans for forty years. But even considering all the red tape, all the publication and bonding procedures, all the many exact resolutions, all the inspections and payments and reporting, it has been shown to be impossible to improve on an interest rate of only three plus percent. Further, government provisions allow for land and services and parking and landscaping. Taken all together, we now know that we never could have built what we did with any other financing — unless, of course, a donor had given the money!

What would nonprofit organizations have done without government surplus? By the time I entered the picture, much of our day-to-day equipment had been obtained as war surplus — desks, typewriters, waste-baskets, paint, carbon paper, and nails. As time progressed and we were distanced from a major war, the available stocks diminished, although in 1956 we did get a used Chevrolet truck from the Navy.

Because grants from the National Science Foundation were primarily attached to research, George Fox had not been able to take advantage of their matching grants. We needed teaching equipment far more. Being in Washington, D. C., in August of 1965, I called in at the office of the National Foundation and learned of two changes which eventually worked to our advantage. One was their decision to allow greater flexibility in the nature of their grants to include teacher grants. The other was to include NASA equipment in the surplus because used hardware and software had come to assume gigantic proportions, filling acres of warehouse space. By this time our faculty had increased in number and had more time to prepare data for applications, and private funds were available to match the federal programs so we benefited from these providential changes.

From 1966 to 1969 many thousands of dollars worth of equipment for the natural and physical sciences, teaching tools for education and psychology, audio and visual aids, and books were added. This is not to say that every whim was gratified. We faced refusals and reversals, sending in petition and protests on many subjects. We lost out on thousands of dollars for Calder Center. Our 1966 applications for library books and Title IV assistance for teachers were both denied. By and large, however, provisions became more generous, we developed more finesse in application, and it came about that we may have gotten more than the average small college.

I have previously alluded to loans for students. We also qualified on a limited basis for the state's scholarship program. In 1965 and 1966 we received federal work-study money, hiring students in the summer for campus work, sending them out as specialists to summer camps, and adding to our scholarship grants for those coming from low income families.

*I*F I WERE WRITING this next section in 1959 instead of 1968, my observations would be diametrically reversed. I am now ready to admit that alumni are the greatest source of support—but this has not always been so. From what we have been able to glean from dozens of sources, the alumni situation at Pacific and George Fox is atypical. Classes have been so small that little or no competitive spirit was ever manifested. There had never been any enthusiastic homecoming spirit—no raccoon coats, no "rah, rah's," no parades for the "class of 1925," no rivalry where one class paid for a bigger memorial than another. As far as records show, no group of alumni had ever gathered and done anything for the alma mater. Until the dedication of Shambaugh Library, there was no marker anywhere on campus of any lasting value. What is obvious at other colleges was completely absent at George Fox.

It was thus difficult to know where to begin with any kind of alumni organization (other than an executive committee), any competition or response, any grouping. These frustrations were shared by one and all, and are not to be taken as mine alone. Leading alumni were discouraged and embarrassed. A major section composed primarily of those graduating or attending in the twenties and thirties was "lost" to the college. Former students from the forties and fifties were often found to be outright antagonistic—the college had let them down. Why get excited about loyalty and support?

I made it a practice to get in touch with alumni in every way possible. I called them on the phone in distant cities when I found myself in nearby railway stations or hotels or airports. I wrote to them. I took them out to lunch. I met them in churches, at civic and fraternal clubs. I called at their homes and offices. Looking back, surely all of these genuine and warmhearted contacts must have been rewarding. At least I greatly enjoyed them, although at the time nothing much seemed to be happening. It was like the proverbial water dropping one drop at a time on a stone. The groups were nonexistent. The numbers small. No one donated any money. No one (or so it appeared) was planning to send the next generation to George Fox. There were not many great, not many mighty. Could anything give life to these dry bones?

Mary Sandoz, class of 1937, assumed the office of alumni director beginning in 1959. She knew all of the grads, worked on the directory, arranged and perfected many innovative programs such as better timing of alumni events, reunions, and citations for alumni of fifty-, twenty-five-, and ten-year classes. She organized the alumni college, instituted the alumnus-of-the-year award, and maintained an orderly file and mailing list. She attended regional and national meetings of the American Alumni Council, greatly broadening her horizon and increasing her effectiveness.

We now know that there is a cumulative effect in which one success leads to another. The college arrives at a milestone, chalks up a new accomplishment, achieves some eminence, and the result is that the alumni assume revived pride in their school. Attendance at alumni affairs, once numbering a dozen or so, climbed into the hundreds. Families, once indifferent and noncommittal, began sending their young people to George Fox — the second, third, and even the fourth generation.

Alumni chapters now function in many areas, with varied success, sometimes carrying on sequel programs, then lapsing into inactivity. In the mid-fifties, we started chapters in Newberg, Salem, Southern Idaho, Eugene, and Seattle. We enjoyed great success in attendance in southern California. In the sixties, we met several times in or near Chicago and twice in Washington, D. C. The southern Washington State group divided into the two centers of Vancouver and Camas, and several important meetings were held annually in southern Oregon. Seattle took on new life again in 1964, and a small group met in New York City in the spring of 1967.

Alumni are the backbone of any financial drive. Eighteen members, all from classes prior to 1920, allowed their names to be used to create a Committee on Estates in 1961. The names read like a hall of fame:

Hervey Hoskins: '99, Chair	Carrie Turner Wortman, '04
Myrtle Bell, '06	Ruth Romig Hull, '06
Tom Benson, '15	Dr. Eunice Lewis, '05
H. S. Britt, '97	Perry Macy, '07
Jessie Britt, '99	Dr. Walter R. Miles, '06
Edwin H. Burgess, '09	Nellie Paulson Moore, '07
E. Worth Coulson, '05	Amos Stanbrough, '93
Leonard George, '10	Elsie Wilson, '08
Ernest Hadlock, '09	Arthur K. Wilson, '08

Some served by chairing committees. Others assumed leadership by virtue of service on the Board of Trustees. The service of dozens, even hundreds, of others assumed significant stature in the constituent churches as pastors, superintendents, counselors to youth, Sunday school teachers, camp directors, and Christian parents.

We have found that alumni give a dramatic boost as a challenge to others by making timely and sizable contributions. The fact that an *alumnus* gives $100,000 is shown to have greater impact than if a similar amount were donated by an impersonal foundation or a government agency. Some of the estates of deceased graduates are worth ten times their monetary value in the enthusiasm and goodwill they inspire, influencing others to remember their alma mater in their wills. Alumni are the key to public relations in every specific. If former students do not support the school that gave them a start, how can it be expected that others, without a personal interest, will rise up to carry on the work? On the other hand, if loyal alumni come forward, a chain of events is set in motion that positively impacts the college for many years.

With small graduating classes, year after year numbering eight to fifteen (in 1955 there were six), it takes years to gain momentum. Beginning with the class of 1966, we began graduating fifty and more in a given year. When a group of that size attends an alumni banquet, joining the association en masse and making a gift to the cause, the alumni from previous years are pleased to say the least; they are proud. There is every reason to believe that a new generation is coming forward to assume the privileges and obligations. There will be a future. There will always be a George Fox College!

Involvement with alumni is a two-way street. It is not exclusively an attempt to extract funds! In fact, as any of our alumni leaders will testify, there has been a change of emphasis. What service can the college render?

There are many possibilities. We have tried a number of them and implemented some successful programs with the association. One is through the Alumni Newsletter, an occasional publication. Another is the Alumni College, a half-day on Saturday of Commencement weekend in which graduates return and "go to college." Lectures or demonstrations, concerts and tours, showing off the newest facilities, have been the bill of fare to date. We initiated a placement service, and while the dossiers of every person are not complete, it has been a good resource for alumni who are involved.

ANOTHER INNOVATION is development of a policy for conferring honorary degrees, not practiced until it was adopted by the board in 1961. Over the years, our leadership had maintained a conservative attitude for which all of us are now thankful. Previously, only two persons had ever been so recognized. The Honorable Herbert Hoover was given a doctorate in 1941 — a bronze plaque in Wood-Mar Hall commemorates the occasion. In 1956, the executive committee and I discussed a problem facing an alumnus, the Reverend Lloyd Creseman, who had been elected to the presidency of Friends University, not having an earned doctorate. His stature suggested an honorary from every point of view, and as his alma mater, it was our prerogative to bestow it. After due deliberation, he was granted a Doctor of Divinity degree.

In 1961 when Professor Mary Sutton had served a full fifty years on the faculty, a committee studied the matter, as did the board, with the following policy being adopted:

> It is the policy of George Fox College to award honorary degrees to such a person or persons who have earned distinction in an area of service so as to merit such an honor. It should be understood that such degrees are conferred in recognition of outstanding service, whether in pastoral, missionary, educational, business or other fields of service, and as a testimony and recognition to those who have made a great contribution to the Christian cause by their witness and work for our Lord and his kingdom.

> It should be further understood that such a policy is not inconsistent with the Quaker concept of "titles and honors" as improper for Christians. It is our position that such an honor should be earned as much as any other degree which we as a college confer, and that it is right and proper to humbly recognize and honor such distinction when it can and will be for the glory of God and his kingdom.

Mary Sutton was granted the Honorary Doctor of Letters degree at commencement in 1961. The next to be so honored were: John Astleford, class of 1934, veteran missionary to Central America with a Doctor of Divinity; Dr. Wayne Burt of Oregon State University with a Doctor of Science for his outstanding achievements in oceanography; Lowell Edwards, ex 1922, the honorary Doctor of Science for his humanitarian service in the invention and development of the famous heart valve which bears his name; Sidney Collier, formerly local head of the Spaulding Pulp and Paper Company, Doctor of Laws for his enlightened labor policies, management and conservation of natural resources, and service to the college; Ralph Choate, class of 1930, Doctor of Letters for his missionary service to Burundi. We trust that we have honored these worthy recipients. We know they have brought honor to the college.

Chapter three

Accreditation

"*I*F I WERE YOU, Ross, I'd close the doors. There is no future here. Get out while you can." I was listening to a candid and reasoned appraisal of the George Fox situation and potential, and the words made me fighting mad. The man across the desk in my office in August, 1956, was none other than Dr. Paul Davis, roving editor of *The Readers Digest,* and one of the leading consultants in higher education. I have often wondered since if he meant to arouse me to positive action, or if he believed sincerely in what he was saying that hot and dry afternoon.

His stated opinion was illustrative of the views of many responsible persons at the time among friend and foe alike, and I have never held it against him for his judgment. I only whistled in the dark and refused to admit his correctness and veracity! Some said it out loud; others kept their thoughts to themselves. Had not Dr. Gervais Carey, president from 1947 to 1950, advanced the proposition that the school should pull in its horns and confine its program to a lower division, junior college status? Had not Spencer George, a trustee, memorialized Oregon Yearly Meeting of Friends Church in a policy paper which included the knell: "and trying to operate a college which we have no business attempting and which we can ill afford"? He resigned from the board a few months later. Had not my close friend and brother, Walter Lee, a trustee and former vice president of the college, written me in all sincerity, "We have

gotten along without the school before. We can do it in the future"?
These men represented a sizable body of opinion, perhaps, for all I
knew, a majority opinion of those who looked to the college. Was
the struggle worth it? Was there hope for the future? Could we
mount the enthusiasm, the expertise, the resources, to challenge the
Northwest Higher Commission and eventually achieve regional
accreditation?

Coupled with the statements and opinions of associates and
peers was a substantial residue of honest fear of accreditation. Some
of the fear came out of the Bible school era in which accreditation,
impossible for the non-liberal arts college, was equated with infi-
delity, liberalism, and kindred evils. I recall sermons in my youth
wherein the minister would give illustrations of unacceptable texts
in science being forced onto erstwhile faithful schools in order for
them to be standardized. It was simple to prove: the colleges which
had denied the old faith were accredited; those which were true
to the gospel were non-accredited. Accreditation, per se, was the
"enemy of the church." Thus, the very aim and goal of acceptance
into the legitimate family of colleges was open to serious question.
As a fellow president of a Christian college put it, "We choose
rather to be good than accredited!"

But I never succumbed to this philosophy. It never rang true to
my ears — not in my early years when I attended a Bible school, nor
as late as the 1960s when I heard very sincere but misled Christian
educators observe that one or another college had lost its religious
zeal because of accreditation. For one thing, it smacked of too-ap-
parent rationalization. My opinion was and is that colleges may
have diluted their strong witness, or changed their educational
philosophy, or relaxed their student standards, but these changes
were not the result of external, professional pressures on the road
to regional accreditation. The very opposite is true. Accreditation is
recognition of excellence. It is, among other things, a vote of confidence from one's peers that there is integrity of purpose and policy,
and worthwhile achievement. It says that a college knows where it

is going, that it has come far enough in the accomplishment of its stated goals to undergo longitudinal testing, and that there is a reasonable expectation that it can bring together sufficient resources of all kinds to continue the process into the indefinite future. It liberates rather than limits a college. If we wished to be a twentieth-century college and be part of the renewal of the Society of Friends, accreditation was our friend. It was more than a fighting chance; it was based upon observable achievement. Although myths and misunderstandings clouded the popular picture in the minds of many, I knew that my predecessors were all committed to the policy, and that Dr. Pennington, President Gulley, and Dr. Parker had all made serious, if unsuccessful, attempts to become accredited in their day. Also, as far as I knew, the Board of Trustees and the faculty had always been committed to the policy. It was not debatable among the higher echelons of directive and administrative opinion.

ONE OF THE FIRST tasks to which I addressed myself on assuming the presidency on January 4, 1954, was a full study of the history of accreditation and of our positions over the years, both favorable and unfavorable, the reasons for successes or failures, and what should be our modus operandi in the forthcoming months and years. Undergirding my search was the statement of Jesus, "The children of this world are wiser in their generation than the children of light," and while I have no disposition to divide the educational community between the sheep and the goats, the observation became a challenge to excellence. Why should not George Fox College, committed to the finest elements in the Christian tradition, be an example of a spirit of accomplishment which brings honor and glory to the great Teacher himself? Our goal never has been that of institutional, or even corporate or personal aggrandizement in itself, but rather that the Great Commission be fulfilled as completely as possible through our dedication. Surely there are no limitations with God. If there are limitations, do they not stem from our own doubt or disobedience? Should we not challenge the accepted position that greatness and success are not for the followers of the lowly Nazarene? Even from the pragmatic point of view, will not industry and integrity and the stewardship of mind and resources pay off?

The files were adequate and voluminous. In the late teens and twenties, there were two possible routes to take: first was the route coming out of the Department of Commerce with policies dictated by Pacific Academy alumnus, Herbert Hoover. Requirements from Washington, D. C., were clear and explicit: modernize and expand the library, and build an endowment of $100,000 (later increased to $200,000). It seemed with the official climate as it was and with a prominent friend in the department, the route of national acceptance was the one to pursue. President Pennington pursued it in a highly successful manner. Money came in by the tens of thousands of dollars from Northwest Quakers, as well as from Philadelphia and England—both of which still viewed Oregon and Pacific College as mission points.

By the 1930s, national accreditation went into bureaucratic limbo, and (officially, at least) all was lost. History was to show that the route which led via Washington, D. C., was a dead end, but who could have foreseen that turn of events in 1924 when all seemed so promising? Who was to prophesy that the independent route of professional accreditation was to prove the lasting one? This second route, Oregon State "standardization" which gave stability to teacher training for a time in our state fifty years ago has developed into the primary method for a college to be accredited unless special professional certification is required.

The administration of Pacific College did all in its power over many years to pursue the former route before forsaking it in favor of the second. As the associations (Northwest along with others) continued to raise the bar, Pacific found it more and more difficult to meet requirements. There is a school of thought (and I quietly subscribe to it) that it could have become accredited in the 1920s when it ranked well among other colleges, before they had so obviously outstripped it. The disparity grew between the progress of sister colleges and Pacific which battled to pay the faculty a subsistence wage while buildings and equipment, once modestly substantial, slowly deteriorated. Attempts to maintain our position perhaps appeared ludicrous to educational leaders of the day, especially those from state universities and more prestigious colleges, and attempt after attempt was unsuccessful. Sadder yet was a kind of enveloping myopia which shut the eyes of administration, faculty, and Board of Trustees alike to the fact that Pacific College was so deeply substandard — that faculty fellowship and happy student camaraderie are not enough to make a respectable seat of education. But yet one class after another came and went, some highly intelligent people were taught by very able and dedicated faculty, and eternal truths were taught by spiritual giants and caught by some ready youth who have gone out to bless the world. If no other witness is ever made to the oft-quoted idea that it is most difficult to kill a college, let Pacific College during the Great Depression and into the years of World War II be the one. Let it be a demonstration, too, that God answers prayer.

To set the record straight, all the fault was not on the side of the college, and all the blame must not be laid at the feet of penury, ineptitude, or nearsightedness. The Northwest Association was not as fair and equitable as it later proved to be, nor were its criteria and methods as sound then as now. In the words of Dr. Adrian Tieleman, "Regional accreditation was (before 1955) once in grace, always in grace."

It is known that the colleges accredited as far back as 1918 and others in the twenties had never been reexamined, nor had they been required to complete a new self-study. Little or no provision was made for newer or rapidly growing colleges to apply for accreditation. Inconsistencies marked whatever directives were made, and subsequent teams of inspection did not work with agreed upon criteria, nor did they transmit to their successors the results of former visits. In fact, genuine antipathy was shown to applicants, the motto being, "We have enough colleges already!"

Twice during the administration of President Emmett Gulley serious attempts were made to achieve accreditation. The first attempt resulted in a directive that a new gymnasium was required. This was reasonable and necessary as anyone in or out of the college would have had to admit. So a campaign was launched to finance and construct an acceptable gymnasium costing some $40,000, tapping all the resources and ingenuity of the constituency in the convulsive years immediately following World War II. The task was completed and Hester Memorial Gymnasium dedicated; the Higher Commission was notified, and a second team appeared. They came and went, leaving a new set of demands, but never once recognizing completion of the new gymnasium! Candor must admit that the academic program during the second evaluation was so slipshod that it took precedence over the new building, but even so, the appalling lack of continuity by visiting committees, and the lack of communication, made it virtually impossible, even for stronger colleges than Pacific, to attain the goal.

My reaction, after having read and reread all the papers extant from that era, and later (even in 1964) having talked to the living members of these first visiting committees, was to find myself torn between a sense of embarrassment occasioned by the naivete and lack of educational understanding evidenced by previous leaders of the college, and outright anger at the lack of courtesy and consideration demonstrated so flagrantly by members of the educational establishment.

After the second visit from the Higher Commission, procedures leading to a proposal were abandoned until the era of Dr. Paul P. Parker. A simple study was undertaken and presented for review by the Higher Commission in 1952. The paper was almost entirely the personal work of the president. It was a very short and terse document, about one-tenth the volume of the self-study which resulted in preliminary accreditation in 1959. Naturally, it got nowhere. Not only was there a lack of institutional direction and comprehension of the field of higher education; even more appalling was a questionable glossing over of conditions inside the college. To such questions as, "Do you consider your physical plant adequate to support the academic needs of the college?" a ready "yes" followed. The same to a question referring to the accessions of the library. The same concerning scientific equipment and paraphernalia. Then there followed a series of questions dealing with the buildings and their appurtenances, and to one and all, with hardly a sobering qualification, the response was a cheerful affirmative! I have no excuse or answer to the outrage.

In the summer of 1954 and into the academic year following, a year's self-study was undertaken. We were very fortunate in both of the consultants who would assist us in the process. The first was Dr. S. A. Gilfillan, Dean of the Graduate School of Science at Oregon State University. Part of the time he served as chair of the Higher Commission. The second, named on Gilfillan's retirement, was Dr. Roy Lieuallen, President of Oregon College of Education and subsequently Chancellor of the Oregon State System of Higher Education.

Of course, we were all woefully ignorant of the scope of the impending self-study, but during the first four years, we accomplished two major goals. The first was to set our house in order and collect and collate data essential to the full report to be submitted and defended at a later date. The second accomplishment was attendance at the annual meetings of the Higher Commission. In so doing, I came to know most of the members of the Commission on a casual, first-name basis. I conferred with Dr. Kerr whenever possible, as well as Father A. A. Lemieux, President of Seattle University, who was elected as chair of the Commission near the end of our self-study, and who presided when we were finally accepted at the Spokane meeting. Even more important, I later realized, were the impromptu encounters at regional and national conventions. For instance, I enjoyed a happy visit with Father Lemieux in St. Louis when we were both attending the annual sessions of the Association of American Colleges.

Sometimes these coffee hours were not all that I hoped they would be. I recall at one meeting of the Northwest Association, Dr. John Riley, President of Northwest Nazarene College at Nampa, Idaho, and a member of the Higher Commission, invited me out to breakfast. I had assumed that he was my friend, but he took the occasion to suggest that we drop the application for accreditation and close the doors to George Fox College. I was never more astounded in my life. Needless to say, I did not take his advice! He continued to be a Christian gentleman to me in public, but I have never understood whether his advice was prompted by pressures he knew were against us in the professional community, or he, like Paul Davis, used the device to spur me to greater effort. Perhaps as a good Nazarene, he honestly wanted, out of self-interest, to rid himself and his college of real or imagined competition. On another occasion, Dr. Paul Smith, president of Whittier College representing the Western Association, took the opportunity of our chance meeting over coffee to take me to task about our publicity, using the terms "evangelical" and "Friends College of the West," et cetera which appeared to him to be unethical. The conversation did clear up some other tensions and misunderstandings, and out of it we had a meeting of minds which gave me and the college openings in southern California to candidate for students, appoint trustees, and enter Friends churches freely.

I soon learned that the field of higher education can be perilous. I realized, as a consequence, that I had to fight in my own right for my college, my position, and myself even. Case in point: when petitions and progress reports were requested, I was told by Dr. Kerr to send sufficient copies to all members of the Commission in care of Father Lemieux, who in turn would distribute them to his associates. One year it seemed propitious to emphasize the size of our invested endowment, which was then and had been for many years, a source of strength. I sent ample copies to Father Lemieux. Then appearing before the Commission, I spoke informally to buttress the written facts and figures—which I assumed had been studied by the members previously. But I soon realized that I did not have the attention of the group, and that there was no comprehension of what I was trying to impress upon them. In a flash, I broke into my talk and addressed the chair: "Father, may I ask if all the members of the Commission have seen my report on the subject?"

"Of course; I gave them out when we first convened." Silence.

"Then, sir, what may the packet contain on the floor behind you?" I asked, after I had assured myself that they were heaped together along with other papers. The good Father had them distributed and I continued my remarks, lifting out salient points, and making my points to advantage. I have since accepted the position that he had actually forgotten my reports, but even so, I have also wondered if George Fox would have progressed as smoothly up to final acceptance if I had not taken the proverbial "bull by the horns." All later reports went first class and airmail to all members individually.

BUT TO GET BACK to the beginning of things in 1955, the process of preparation proved to be a long and tedious one. And here, as elsewhere in the area of administration, the problem of going back to former years to lift out data, to try to get answers when it appeared the answers were not readily available, to sift out conflicting materials, to make assignments to research, was ever with us. From the vantage point of these later years, my attitude has mellowed materially, so that I have sympathy for previous administrators especially from the 1930s to 1950s who, because of lack of personnel, were forced to leave so many items on the agenda undone. There were years without trained librarians. There were many years with part-time bookkeepers. Until 1956 the college had never boasted a full-time development officer except during a campaign. The position of dean was not filled until 1949 and even then with teaching assignments as well. There were no directors of testing or counseling or health or development or research or federal relations.

However, when a school begins to gird itself for a self-study and the meaning of crucial questions in a volume of criteria for accreditation becomes all too clear, the administration is forced, at long last, to go back to former years to pick up the broken strands; to project backward from the present to the immediate and more remote past; to simulate, to create, and sometimes to recreate. In a word, the very fact that valuable data had not been kept, to say nothing of kept up-to-date, finally catches up. It cannot be ignored. Dr. Arthur Roberts took on the arduous task of bringing current the alumni directory The last attempt had been in 1935. He was later joined in the task by Mary Sandoz, but it took them four years from inception to printing.

Financial records were in much the same state, although what was not down in writing was in the head of Oliver Weesner who was treasurer and head bookkeeper, a member of the investment committee, trustee of the yearly meeting, surveyor, and professor of mathematics for thirty years! Richard Kneeland, whose firm took over the auditing during President Gulley's tenure, admitted to me that he found the account books as much as six years in arrears. It seemed to all of us that no project could be taken on, let alone completed satisfactorily, without a great deal of research into old books, delving into safes, and always trips to the dusty but ample attic of Wood-Mar Hall.

I have mentioned the alumni files and general finances. These, although highly important, were only two of the subjects in question. I took on the area of administration and much of the research relating to the aims and goals of the college. Dean Kenneth Williams assisted me with the latter as well as student services and academic programs. We worked through the summers, especially in 1958 and 1959. In retrospect, our greatest difficulty came from the faculty who, having been given an assignment relating to their field or major or classes, would not finish their work by the end of the term in June, and Williams and I would spend the next weeks telephoning or writing them—or even visiting them on their vacation or in summer school.

Further, the differences in format and literary style compelled us to do a thorough job of reediting all submitted copy. But first one page and then another fell into place. It grew and grew, and although now it does not look as professional as later editions and it suffers by contrast with subsequent volumes, we were proud of it at the time. It was neat. It was accurate. It was complete. But above all, it was boldly honest! We admitted to the full roster of inefficiencies, inadequacies, and limitations. We delineated where our buildings were dilapidated and obsolete, our library offerings were weak, our science equipment incomplete or outmoded. We admitted to a small constituency base, to a small alumni organization, to problems stemming from poor heating and plumbing. We admitted that our student housing was minimal. All the same, we highlighted every favorable development or condition possible. We accentuated the positive. We showed graphically the strength of the endowment, the growing support from the church, the $25,000 raised by the city of Newberg, all the foundation support we had gained. We showed the faithfulness of the faculty and its low turnover. We highlighted the accomplishments of the alumni from Herbert Hoover forward. We demonstrated with full evidence every type of progress that could be shown. We displayed our long-range planning, our innovation and experimentation, our search for qualified young scholars, the calibre of our trustees—all this and more. A spirit of progressive optimism pervaded the entire book. When one reads it, even today, one cannot escape the feeling that George Fox is a legitimate college and that it has a future.

Following submission of the formal report, our fate hung on two more decisions—the visit and vote of the committee, and its report to and the final action of the Higher Commission itself. Much could be written about these sessions, but I shall limit myself to one or two episodes. No doubt each professor, each student, each trustee who was present for the visit considered his or her interview significant, and each one was, building to an impressive crescendo on the final afternoon. The major interview in my office, lasting some two hours, took an interesting turn, and I have elected to comment on it.

Father Howard Kenna, the amiable president of the University of Portland, was the chair, accompanied by Dean Kerr. The questions and discussion centered primarily on the Christian philosophy of education adhered to and advanced by George Fox. In this, as well as in other matters, I had an ally in Father Kenna, and I am sure that I made my points. This led eventually to the matter of commitment, academic freedom, and the possibility and probability of candidating and holding a faculty and staff with interests consonant to the stated aims of the college. For, in the words of Father Kenna, "In my opinion, if George Fox cannot maintain a faculty loyal to its unique Christian ideals, it might as well become a public institution."

One of my deepest concerns, even before assuming the presidency, was whether a college such as George Fox could capture the imagination of keen scholars—true to the faith—who would strive for excellence in preparation for their chosen professions. As far back as 1945, when I was the speaker at a Religious Emphasis Week at Pacific, I had struck a responsive note when I exhorted, "What we need are more sanctified PhDs!" One of my major tasks in these first five years of work was to talk to and correspond with a great number of promising candidates, some still in high school, some among our student body, some among our leading alumni, and others in other colleges or different professions. All this concern and activity stood me in good stead! I went to my files in the presence of these two gentlemen and lifted out a thick folder marked "Prospects." I did not have to go through it. I did not need to defend each and every person. The very fact that I was engaged in the search—that we had a policy—carried the day. The drama of little things may mean more than reasoned arguments.

I recall a conversation from my appearance before the Higher Commission itself. One of the subjects on the table was the career success of alumni. What percentage has gone on to graduate work? How many are illustrious or famous? How do the accomplishments of these former students rank with the historic aims of the institution? Again, our attention to detail paid off—51 percent continued on to graduate schools; 52 percent employed in the sacred callings; 92 percent active in church work, et cetera.

But what appears successful to us may not impress other educators, especially if they are not imbued with Christian zeal. The small number of alumni, totaling less than twelve hundred, (smaller than one graduating class of institutions represented by the presidents and deans sitting before me) forced me into a defensive maneuver. Dr. S. A. Eastvold, president of Pacific Lutheran College (now University) came to my rescue. "How many of us have produced a president of the United States? I vote for George Fox," bringing down the house. It was a rhetorical question which should not be answered because the accomplishments of 1891 have little bearing on 1959, but what he did carried the day and I shall always be grateful. A combination of Jesuits and Lutherans voted in the Quakers!

I had read the report of the committee which was favorable in its majority opinion. In it I found a number of ways to strengthen our position before the next cycle of review. I assumed these had been read and debated by the Higher Commission. But when the favorable decision of the Higher Commission was handed down, we noticed that we were granted accreditation with suggestions different from those of the committee. Some were diametrically opposite. Thus we learned that the Higher Commission is the final authority—their recommendations were the ones to address. This first accrediting critique is as follows:

> Following the presentation of the reports, the committee discussed at length the problem of accreditation. Attention was drawn to the remarkable improvement in the past few

years under Dr. Ross as president and to the fine spirit of cooperation which the faculty and staff had manifested. The opinion and the consequent vote of the committee was not unanimous, but the majority voted to recommend to the Higher Commission that unrestricted accreditation be given to George Fox College for a period of two years subject to a progress report at the end of the first year and a further progress report at the end of the second year.

Respectfully submitted,

Howard J. Kenna, C. S. C.

The Higher Commission later concurred with the committee's report.

When I was met in the hall later by members coming out of the closed session and given a favorable sign, I was so depleted that I staggered off to my hotel room in thankful relief. I telephoned the college. I prepared a victory statement for the student body, and when Dean Williams and I arrived back at the college, I read it before the excited student body and faculty. School was out for the day. A big parade serpentined down First Street, the victory bell ringing for an hour or more.

We were first accredited for two years, through the 1961 meeting of the Northwest Association. Claude Simpson, registrar at Washington State University, chaired the second committee, and we were granted a full extension of three years, up to 1964. The new buildings and other factors showed that we had kept faith and that we were a much stronger institution. The official report signed by Simpson extended accreditation for three additional years.

Sentiment was expressed in the Higher Commission by Dr. Earl Crockett of Brigham Young University (who chaired the visiting committee for Cascade College) that we should experiment with a cooperative arrangement between George Fox and Cascade. In fact, there was a long history of attempts at moving toward merger, so that the interest of the Higher Commission was nothing new, and was tolerably congenial to both administrations. The story is so closely tied to the accreditation story of both schools, especially in recent years, that some of the salient facts should be told here and in chapter 5.

CASCADE CHRISTIAN COLLEGE (formerly Portland Bible Institute) was founded in 1918 as a result of a holiness movement against the leadership of President Levi Pennington. Quaker leaders, especially Lewis I. Hadley, Jay Sherman, Jay Cook, Lavena Terrell, and later Edward Mott, Sophia E. Townsend, and Elizabeth Ward, were active in the movement. The school began holding classes in the rented basement of Piedmont Friends Church in north Portland. Evidence subsequent to the heat of the early years seems to suggest that excesses were committed by both sides, but that if President Pennington had hired some of these wonderful Bible teachers onto his faculty, there need never have been another school which, for the Friends at least, divided loyalties and dissipated stewardship for two generations.

It is not for me to question any of the stalwarts of the faith of fifty years ago. Surely, the Bible school and the later liberal arts college rendered stellar service to the kingdom of God, especially in the area of missions, and more recently to the leadership of the Evangelical United Brethren Church. I attended there as a boy out of high school, and I am glad that I did. I was invited onto the faculty in 1936, but turned down the offer. My alma mater conferred upon me an honorary doctorate in 1958, for which I am greatly indebted. On three or four subsequent occasions I was considered for the presidency by at least vocal and responsible segments of the leadership. I served three years as chancellor of the three schools—George Fox, Cascade College, and Warner Pacific—after the formation of the Associated Christian Colleges of Oregon. But to resume.

Cascade was a respected institution of higher learning, and leaders such as Dr. C. J. Pike, Dr. Earl Barker, Dr. Phillip Clapp, and Dr. Ray Nash were in the top echelon of Christian educators. For my part, and for whatever it may mean to this narrative, I highly respected President Pike. Although I did not take to his methods in a number of instances when we clashed over the years, anyone who can take a wobbly, little Bible school and develop it into a strapping, vigorous city college of 300 students without dependable support, based solely on adherence to unpopular religious tenets, has my admiration. Dean Gilfillan, while serving as our consultant, held up Cascade College as an example for us to follow.

But an independent private college with a self-perpetuating board, without the strength of denominational control, and operating on a limited educational philosophy, rises or falls on the dynamic leadership (or lack of it) of one man. After twenty successful years in the presidency, Dr. Pike resigned and the institution he worked so hard to build began to fall apart—ever so slowly at first, but noticeably to those of us close enough to see, and then with increasing momentum until in one twelve month period in 1966-67, four different presidents came and went in rapid succession. The last one, Mr. Nate Olson, after only five months at the helm, was informed that accreditation was being withdrawn. It is a terrible thing to see a good college disintegrate. It had been running on the momentum of its former heyday. Its strongest professors, left one after another. In the light of rising costs and falling income; great complicated tasks and fewer capable people to carry them out; finances in an impossible, incomprehensible jumble; its leaders (I trust innocently) depending upon highly questionable procedures; a person from the Seattle office of Health, Education, and Welfare confided to one of our staff in 1967, "We have come to accept the figures in Cascade's papers as pure fabrication."

However, not all of this dreary recital had come about when the Higher Commission began its interest in our cooperation, and certainly the more glaring problems were not known to the members. What was known was that some unfruitful discussions were held by Cascade's Dr. Pike and our Dr. Parker in 1951. Later, I recall perhaps eight or ten sessions from 1957 to 1965 with members of the administration, and some five or six called meetings with our board and their board. The George Fox contingent became increasingly critical of the feasibility of involvement in anything which smacked of a true merger because in most instances the Cascade board failed to communicate its position officially; as often as not the recommendations of the administration were not put into effect by the board in session; and some members of the Cascade board seemed to aspire to control without accepting the more demanding role of support. As time wore on to the sad summer of 1967, it became apparent that there was nothing to salvage — there was nothing to merge.

All the same, we were having our own financial problems stemming from an unfavorable teacher-student ratio, especially at the upper-division level, and both of us were in the unhappy situation that some excellent professors were being exposed to too few students. Academic cooperation was a logical solution even if legal merger was not. It began on a limited basis with Cascade in 1964 and with Warner Pacific College as early as 1963.

Warner Pacific and George Fox found an easy affinity. Under the strong patronage and support of the Church of God (Anderson, Indiana) its presidents and faculty had close harmony with us in many respects; its candidating was at a high level, and its social standards were the same as ours. While Cascade allowed a lax situation to develop, Warner ran a tighter ship year by year, strengthened its program, and made rapid progress. We followed the advice of the Higher Commission and, while the three institutions moved closer academically, another force precipitated an early association. I speak of teacher training.

ACCREDITATION BY THE Northwest Association is *overall*, institutional accreditation. Teacher training at all levels, on the other hand, must be accredited by the Oregon State Department of Education because teaching is considered professional and specialized. A team from each of the two agencies would be involved — the Northwest Association observing and evaluating the total operation, and the Oregon Department of Education giving direct attention to education and the subject matter fields for which a college is training teaching candidates. We were advised to take these projects on separately. Thus, when we were first accredited in 1959, we did not achieve accreditation for our education majors to teach in the state of Oregon. We considered the institutional accreditation to be the foundation for approval for a specialized program—that the one would give us an advantage to pursue the second. We were to find ourselves in a morass of interdepartmental intrigue, bickering, and bias which may be difficult to believe could happen in enlightened America. But therein hangs my tale! Some background is necessary to appreciate our situation and the general problem which has hung over Oregon schools for many years.

For many years Oregon law provided for the training of public school teachers in a dual-track system. The state normal schools had a legal monopoly on elementary training up through the eighth grade. They also trained for high schools (secondary), but not exclusively. Private liberal arts or specialized teacher training schools were allowed to conduct programs for this field—subject, of course, to observation and licensure.

Pacific College was involved in the secondary program over most of its years. In the 1890s to the early 1900s, we provided teachers at all levels and our record in the field was highly commendable. Later, regulations changed and we continued at the secondary level only. Standardization in the 1930s and 1940s took care of provisions for certification of our candidates. This appears to have been a good period with a majority of our graduates going into the profession. Our teachers not only acquitted themselves with honor in the classroom, but many went on to hold positions in administration, to earn their doctorates, and to become successful at colleges and universities.

After this time, two inexorable movements operated against Pacific: first, both national and state agencies raised their standards, and second, although painful to admit, our school did not. Rather, we regressed.

Our enrollment grew in the late 1940s and candidates came on apace, however, it was the ill fortune of these graduates to find themselves without an accredited degree, often with unacceptable credits, lacking full credentials to teach. Even during these most difficult last twenty years, 52 percent of our students have gone on in educational fields, often with costly extra years of added preparation and loss of salary and status. I have found that the disappointments coming out of these problems have been the single greatest hurdle yet to achieving full alumni loyalty. In the same way, these questions and misunderstandings, along with the bonafide problems of actual accreditation for teacher training, have been the single greatest hindrance to student enrollment and retention.

Every possible legitimate device has been used by the college and by our teacher graduates themselves to circumvent rules, to justify their status, to earn certification. For a period of years, it was the practice to take additional summer school classes at a state teacher's college, thus meeting the provisional requirement by autumn in time to teach. This plan was legal for both elementary and secondary teachers, other credits being satisfactory, but as the requirements changed, it applied only to elementary. Then candidates were required to take a full, extra year at a state college.

What has been written up until now refers to our graduates and candidates for the state of Oregon only. Through different state laws and department regulations, and various reciprocity agreements, our students could achieve certification almost anywhere easier than at home! The Portland school system, being a law unto itself, proved to be a haven, taking and keeping our teachers on their own merits. So also the states of Idaho, Montana, Nevada, Colorado — all of these before we achieved the Northwest accreditation. When we passed that milestone, however, we made official overtures to both California and Washington, and while each had its own unique regulations, we found the officials both cooperative and eager, and in a matter of only months we had the processes agreed upon for the certification of our secondary candidates. The state of Alaska was desperate for qualified teachers at all levels and paid high salaries. The conflict inside the state of Oregon meant nothing to them and they were only too pleased to have our graduates, armed as they were with an accredited degree.

Following World War II and into the Korean War, Oregon found itself desperately short of certified public school teachers and the rules must have been relaxed in various ways to fill job openings. One of the better schemes was legislation bringing the private liberal arts colleges into existing programs of elementary training.

The law provided that the accredited colleges of Oregon could enter upon a contractual arrangement with any of the three state teachers' colleges wherein the four year liberal arts school offered a directed program for the first three years, the candidate matriculating following a fourth year at the teacher's college. It was called a "joint degree" program, because both schools conferred a degree — the liberal arts school a bachelor of arts or science by transferring back the fourth year onto its records, and the state school a professional degree of bachelor of arts or science in education by accepting the first three years. With the latter came the state certification. The required courses in methodology, state law, and practice teaching were all under state direction. In later years, the volume of requirements grew, so that the first three years on our campus were very controlled and heavy, and it was impossible to finish in a minimum of four years. Most candidates spent a full twelve months at the state school, generally enrolling in the summer immediately following their junior year.

But to get back to the initiation of the program. Previous to our official entrance into the program, a number of our sister schools had signed up, all of which were accredited. Cascade, for instance, had gone this route following its Northwest accreditation in 1949. But it was my happy privilege and honor, as my first official act as president, on Monday, December 5, 1954, to sign the papers legalizing our joint degree program with Western Oregon College of Education. The circumstances leading up to this event were most satisfying to me personally.

Our candidates had long been associated with the Monmouth college, petitioning their way through in extra years or by a series of summer schools. They had made good in most instances. In fact, some had been so outstanding that their accomplishments reflected most favorably not only on to Western Oregon College of Education, but back onto Pacific or George Fox, which had been responsible for most of their training. The good professors at WOCE saw the inequity of our situation, even if the officers in Salem could not, and decided to liberalize the requirements with George Fox in a bilateral manner. Dr. Floyd Albin was authorized to proceed. Floyd and I were lifelong friends from early Salem school days, and it proved to be one of the most warmhearted series of conferences imaginable for both of us. He had heard of my election to the presidency that spring and had left no stone unturned to effect an official agreement at the earliest moment. George Fox was the first and only college in the state ever to be so recognized before it was regionally accredited!

What a boon it has proved to be ever since. All of our candidates for elementary teaching began to use this legal, acceptable, and swift route. Every year since, a group has graduated from both colleges. Some have made outstanding records, which has brought solidarity to the program and made it easy for continuation when it has been necessary to review the agreement every few years. From the viewpoint of George Fox, the only internal problem has been that we have lost the student body leadership and the tuition of the seniors who must attend Monmouth. Positively though, they have been challenged from high school on to accept the George Fox program in elementary education, and they become an active segment of our alumni association.

In the meantime, we have made every effort and extended our resources enormously to gain approval at the secondary level. What a rocky road it has been — full of many forced stops and starts, with detours leading up to dead ends!

In the late 1950s Dean Kenneth Williams served as a professor of education and his public school background equipped him to work with the state program. While we were not applying for state approval in a formal way, he endeavored to keep abreast of legal developments and personnel changes in Salem. He kept up his personal contacts, took direction from various members of the staff, and invited different leaders of the state system to speak in education classes and chapel and keep us on track toward more formal procedures. We came to realize, after a number of shattering experiences, that we were the victim of departmental rivalries, changes of regulations, interpretations, and new laws. When we took the direction of one person, we were to find it reversed by peers, superiors, or successors. The following are illustrative of the obstacles we encountered for the next several years up until 1966.

We felt it was appropriate to give the students all the accoutrements of status short of formal recognition, so the dean sponsored a student society for cadet teachers attached to the Oregon Education Association. The students carried on their meetings with enthusiasm and attended state-wide councils. Two of them, Maynard Corlett and Janice Bishop, even ran for state office. In order to take advantage of professional leadership for the students and at the same time seek to impress the Salem people, Dr. Dick Sorick, Assistant Superintendent of Certification, was invited to speak before the monthly meeting of the club. Full attendance greeted his arrival in the old library. He used the occasion to degrade George Fox as an institution, ridiculing his audience for having been so foolish as to attend in the first place, and took away their charter in the state organization. It was a tremendous breach of professional courtesy. Dean Williams was furious, and at the same time appalled. All of his well-laid plans had gone by the board.

So we came at the matter from another approach. Dr. Sorick went his way and was replaced, and the only thing to do was to begin to work with his successor. He advised that a program of practice teaching should be initiated at the secondary level, citing state regulations and pointing out that an ongoing, observable program would need to be functioning in order for a committee to observe. This seemed to be the breakthrough we needed.

Newberg school district superintendant Loran Douglas was approached and he was in favor of the proposal. In a few weeks the board of the college signed an agreement with the school district to affect the legal program. I will say to the credit of all—our board, the school board, Mr. Douglas, Dean Williams, our professors, the master teachers in the public school system, together with the students chosen to participate in the pilot year—that everything went off ideally. In fact, Mr. Douglas was so pleased with the program that he was all for an unlimited extension—when the bomb fell from Salem. We had been misadvised. It was illegal for us to carry out such a program, and rather than George Fox being at fault, primarily, the public schools were themselves in jeopardy for having allowed the agreement to be signed in the first place. All must be terminated immediately. Rather than the regulations allowing for our program to be initiated prior to observation leading to state accreditation, all must wait until after accreditation was granted. Yet, accreditation could not be given without a full program, including practice teaching! Something had to be done. Dean Williams and I secured an interview with Dr. Joy Hills Gubser, who was in charge of the certification of teachers in the Oregon system.

We found her to be most capable but completely unapproachable as far as our plight was concerned. We were unable to comprehend the double talk of the state regulations, and asked if there could be a further explanation of them. No go. We asked if the procedures for new schools coming into the program could be spelled out. No go. Later in the discussion about what should be our next move, she responded by advising us to drop the entire matter and desist from any application. She was of the opinion that no school under a thousand students could carry out an acceptable program looking toward state approval. (Here was the seed thought which eventually led us to cooperate with Cascade and Warner Pacific because the combined enrollment of all three came to approximately nine hundred at the time.) Further, she said, "Dr. Ross, I am unalterably opposed to private schools preparing teachers for the public system. If I have my way, there will come a day when only the state colleges will be certified to prepare teachers."

This was a new one! We had undergone various indignities and harassments, having to change our course, but we had not realized that we faced a battle with the highest authorities whose professional bias was completely at variance with ours. I responded by saying that our board and administration were firmly committed to pursuing the policy, and would she be so kind as to advise us what were the next steps. The law allowed us entrance into the program and although we had not made much of it previously, none of the advice we had been given was put in writing and we would appreciate confirmation of oral directives in writing. She gave us some suggestions and true to her word, she later confirmed them. However shocking these revelations were, we forged ahead, and the next weeks and months were fruitful in a number of developments.

I felt it was essential to review our entire policy as an institution. Should we proceed? Did we have the resources in personnel and finance to mount a sustained and excellent program? What really were the demands of the State Department? Joy Gubser had repeatedly told us of a new policy in an impending law which she had proposed to the legislature. The main feature was a five-year basic requirement for the secondary credential, but the stickler was that the college offering the program leading to the credential must offer all five years itself. This would make it impossible for a school to offer an accredited four-year program while depending on another college or university to provide for the final year. A school such as George Fox would be unable to add the fifth year due to funding limitations and disapproval from the Northwest Higher

Commission. Although the measure did not find support in the leg-islature, the threat hung over us for two bienniums.

The subsequent exchange of letters, the comings and goings of bureau people, and added information brought our trustees to a series of far-reaching decisions. The first, and possibly the most important, was the straightforward unanimous vote to proceed at all costs. The preprofessional classes offered were completely con-sonant with our traditional philosophy and offerings for the last sixty years. A vocal majority of our alumni could not be ignored. Present and future student demand prophesied an ever better future. Therefore, forward march!

However, officers in Salem were concerned that our educa-tion department had no home of its own on campus. They felt that education, as a discipline, should not be compromised by being taught in the same building as psychology, English, or history, for instance. Now that we were in the midst of studies leading to the building of a new library, we should be well-advised to separate the education library holdings completely—the general library and the specialized education library should not be in the same building, providing an antiseptic environment for frail education. All of which added up to gloomy discussion of where could we find the finances for a new education center. It seems surprising on occasion how something, altogether apparent, remains obscure and beclouded for so long. There had been some talk about tearing down Kanyon Hall, the old dormitory for women now that the new Pennington Hall was soon to be available. In 1962, Kanyon Hall became the refurbished Minthorn Hall—education center for years to come.

SETTING THE TIME sequence aside for the moment, may I comment further on the subject of the separate location of the education library? In due time, we were put into an inspection calendar, our self-study was completed and submitted the first of September, 1966, and a team of inspectors came to look us over a few weeks thereafter. I am not giving a full report here, but rather only commenting on the libraries. In one of the written suggestions, the subject was brought up for review. Why, said the analysis, with the superb facilities of Shambaugh Library, did we persist in housing our education collection in a separate building? Would we not find it more efficient and economical to have all of our collections in one building, administered by the same professional staff? Would that not render an added service to our students? Indeed!

ONE OF THE most discouraging rulings we faced was that all of our candidates in secondary education who hoped to graduate in June, 1960, (six months after our regional accreditation), obtaining their provisional certificate by attendance at another institution, were now informed that it would be impossible. For all intents and purposes, we as a college and our teacher candidate graduates in particular, were now worse off than before we had achieved regional accreditation. We went to bat. Fighting with every known device and persuasion, we eventually secured a favorable ruling from Joy Gubser to the effect that the young people involved would be given their certificates, but any later graduates (1961 and on) would not. It made us aware that the rules and regulations were subject to one person's whim. No law on the statute books could ever have suffered any such interpretation!

As an aside, it is well known that each state is a law unto itself. Many illustrations could be deduced to show the variety of legislation on the books all over the country, some harsh and stern, and others very lax. As a Quaker college president, I knew of some of these differences as they applied to other colleges in other states. Malone College made the change in the fifties from a Bible college to a full liberal arts college. It would be several years before the North Central Association could grant regional accreditation, but within a very short time after establishing itself and its program in Canton, the Ohio State Department of Education fully certified Malone for teacher training. Much of its rapid growth, and especially the size of its summer school, can be attributed to this happy position. William Penn College was in a different position from either of us, having previously enjoyed both regional accreditation and state teacher training approval. When it was reinstated by the North Central Region, the Des Moines office immediately did the same for the education program, and going further, made it possible for all of the candidates who had graduated in the interim to be certified.

It is easy for a sympathetic student of our problems to understand why some of us came to suffer from a persecution complex. We assumed that little George Fox was having all of the problems but we were not alone—some of our sister schools were having difficulties all their own. Pacific University had been receiving negative reviews, or so the gossip had it. President Mike Ritchey and I had lunch together, going over the situation, and surely enough he felt harrassed and insecure. Cascade College was warned repeatedly. But the big news was the University of Portland. It boasted probably the best and most pretentious program of any private institution in the Northwest. It was large enough, and appeared to have resources to carry on a very sound program leading up to a doctorate in education. All of its programs were fully accredited by the Northwest Association. It went through an educational self-study and review only to have the papers break open an angry exchange of charges and counter charges. President Harry Dillin of Linfield told of his troubles too. Without doubt, George Fox was not the only school facing these difficulties. With counsel from our trustees, I decided to go along with the other presidents in the Oregon Independent Colleges Association.

In due course we met with Superintendent Minear, Dr. Gubser, and members of the State Board of Education. Eugene Fisher, president of the board presided. He graciously told of the contribution that teachers who had their schooling in private colleges had made to his own life. He was very complimentary about those coming from Pacific College. What I did not realize was that Father Paul Waldschmidt had worked not only with the "in" colleges but also with the state leaders to effect the meeting. In one sense, not yet being certified, George Fox was present by deference only. He was given the floor and read a masterful paper about the problems which his university had been facing, but he went further in taking on himself the total issue in the state: the law which granted us the right to be in the field, the principle of freedom for both public and private schools to operate freely, the recent harrassments, the fears under which we all operated, and the resultant deteriorating situation. It was the finest paper of its kind I have ever listened to.

Then one after another, the presidents or deans spoke. All voiced their sentiments, respectfully pointing out the areas at issue as they were reflected at their separate schools. All claimed to have been ill-treated at the hands of the State Department, with the possible exception of the president at Mount Angel. Being on the outside, as it were, there was little in our situation which paralleled the other schools, so when my turn came, it seemed that the only thing which had not been said, and which could help the entire community, was to bring up the matter of professional bias. This I did. I explained the problems faced by all of the independent schools if we were forced to work against personal opposition. I brought out, in a few words, our earlier interview with Joy Gubser. After I finished, she took the floor immediately, hotly denying what she had said in my hearing. Every eye was on me. She glared at me, flushed and angry. Prayerfully, I summoned words and answered: "This is very embarrassing for me and all of us. I am sure I had no intention of arguing with Dr. Gubser. Let us leave the matter this way. If this ever comes to a hearing, I have a witness and I am willing to testify to the truth of what I have said."

Over the next days, I received a number of congratulatory messages in the mail, over the phone, or by personal greeting. So much for the Salem scene for the time being.

WE CONTINUED fully accredited by the Northwest Association up to 1964. By a happy coincidence, it came about that the time for review for George Fox, Cascade, and Warner Pacific was to be the same general date, and the Higher Commission appointed one committee to examine all three schools. Father Leary, president of Gonzaga University, was chair, assisted by a fine group of associates representing different colleges and disciplines. Of course, it goes without saying that we had worked very hard indeed to prepare our self-study. It was Dr. Moore's first with us, and we are still proud of it. The committee came to each of the three schools, then we had individual sessions when they gave us their general evaluations, and finally there was a top-level meeting of the committee with the presidents and deans all at Warner Pacific. The end result was that extension for each of us was recommended, but George Fox came out the strongest.

In the sessions, both publicly and in private, members of the committee exhorted all of us to greater cooperation. None of us was dictated to in the sense of telling us the nature of the cooperation, or how the administrations and their supporting boards were to achieve it, but there was no doubt as to the way the official wind was blowing. We were to get together somehow, and the sooner the better, or else! These recommendations were fully endorsed by the Higher Commission, which made the informal suggestions of the committee all the more important. It would have been folly for us not to have acted in concert and in good faith.

Taking the cue from Joy Gubser about enrollment of a thousand students and the development that Warner Pacific College was making overtures for teacher training arrangements with Portland State College (now University), representatives from the three schools who were present at the Northwest Association meeting in Salt Lake City gathered for a brainstorming session. This was the last week in November, 1964. Out of the discussion, there emerged two plans for action—one was to organize an association embracing the three schools (the emerging Associated Christian Colleges of Oregon), and the other was to engage a team of educational experts to research options for a joint school of education. These informal decisions were shared the next day with members of the Higher Commission, much to their evident satisfaction.

The two men called to conduct the research were Dr. C. Wesley Gaspers of Montana Western College of Education at Dillon, and Dr. Lansing Bulgin of Missouri State Teachers College at Kirksville. Both were able to secure short leaves of absence. Financial arrangements were agreed upon; both men arrived in due time, did their studies, and eventually returned to their home institutions. But a word about each of them.

Gaspers was a member of the Northwest investigating committee and had become interested in the possibilities of educational cooperation. As a member of the Northwest team he could represent that sector and his acquaintance with the National Council for Accreditation of Teacher Education bridged his professional connections acceptably to the Oregon State Department. A quiet, studious fellow, he soon gained the respect of all with whom he worked. In all such appointments, I felt that I should not exclusively choose Quakers or people whom I had known and recommended, and although he had served at Friends University, this was not commonly known in the Northwest—he represented a Montana State college. None of the people suggested by the other presidents became serious candidates. In more than one sense, the initiative and main burden of all of these preliminary considerations came back to me.

Bulgin was another matter. We had known each other much of our lives. His mother had been a teacher at Cascade when it was still a Bible institute. He had attended George Fox and taught part-time back in the forties. His wife, Eleanor, had been a student at Cascade. His former family connections at Cascade made him most acceptable to the Cascade contingent as "their" candidate. He had taught in several schools, but most recently at Kirksville, Missouri. He served there first as a professor on its music faculty, then became the director of curriculum studies, and gave much of his time to the cadet teacher training program, both on campus and in travel to the high schools of the state. Altogether, his background and experience proved to be very impressive. Although not known professionally in the Northwest accrediting circles before coming to the new assignment, his credentials paved the way for him, and he was soon accepted personally by all concerned.

As I have said, both of these leaders were able to arrange to come to the Oregon coast as part of their sabbaticals. Bulgin came first, arriving for duty in February, and stayed on a full three months. Gaspers made two trips, being on duty not more than six weeks altogether, but submitting his papers after preparing them at Dillon.

The men addressed themselves first to the teacher training programs of the three member colleges. Cascade's was the strongest with its secondary program fully accredited by the State Department, and a cordial relationship with the Portland school district in which its practice teaching program was carried on and many of its alumni were employed. Cascade was one of the colleges approved for the joint degree with Oregon College of Education at Monmouth. It was, however, finding itself under the negative scrutiny of the State Department, being repeatedly warned and finding that its extensions were to be shorter and shorter.

George Fox may be considered between the two regarding its teacher training program. Its elementary joint-degree had been established since 1954, but there was no official recognition for secondary. Earlier attempts to gain approval have been alluded to already.

Warner Pacific had no legal status for either elementary or secondary. It had only recently made the transition from a Bible college to four-year liberal arts; it had only within months taken the official position of electing to train in education. Now there was an increasing demand by students. Marvin Lindemuth, academic dean, had been given the task of effecting some change as soon as possible. At the moment, their treatment in Salem was much the same as George Fox only more so, as it was assumed the aura of the Bible college still hung over them and they had no history at all in the field. About this time, they were investigating a cooperative arrangement with the education people at Portland State. Philosophically and practically, Warner had never warmed up to the idea of sending its seniors off to Monmouth, and continued to hope against hope that an affiliation could be effected with an institution in Portland.

In a word, these were the situations of each of the three schools on the arrival of our research consultants. After acquainting themselves with these data, they set about to learn the state education structure — the laws, the regulations, and the people in the Salem and Eugene offices.

The idea of a consortium composed of up to one thousand students was part of their thinking. One thousand students were to be taught by a given number of professors teaching certain courses. Supporting these courses was to be one major education library, or were there to be three? The practice teaching opportunities were to be arranged in one or two or three districts — the Portland system loomed large in their thinking because of Cascade's satisfactory program. The legal structure of a possible tripartite educational entity posed problems. Should George Fox and Warner Pacific come in under Cascade's wing? Or should each carry on separately? Or could the general lower division work of each school be handled by each college individually with the specialized upper division major being at one location? Would the new, emerging ACCO be for education majors only?

Gaspers and Bulgin tried on all of these alternatives "for size." In the course of discussions with Salem in which tentative structures were considered, they were strongly advised to create an entirely new school of education — an entity to be separate from and above the three supporting schools, yet drawing from all three and nurtured by them. The idea was so novel and the implications so great that the resultant reactions were as varied as the people entertaining them. It was pointed out that the state regulations neither exactly allowed nor forbade such an alliance.

As far as I know, Warner Pacific was willing to continue to pursue this course. It had nothing to lose and all to gain. George Fox also was in favor of proceeding. My own reaction tended to be a creative one — why not be the first to branch out into new areas of exploration? We had our difficulties trying to come up with something satisfactory to the state and ourselves, and if now they were showing their goodwill and imagination on our behalf, would we not be obtuse were we to refuse the opportunity? The possibilities were all the more alluring with the professional rapport achieved by our team.

But these attitudes and reactions were not entertained by Cascade. They had an approved program, now of many years' good standing, and any suggestion to fit into an unknown, novel three-way arrangement loomed as a threat — and not without evident justification. The Cascade program, even with some internal weaknesses discovered by examining committees, was still a genuine program; it enjoyed full state approval; its graduates went out fully certified; its connections with the Portland school district were most amicable. They were wary of an alliance with both George Fox and Warner Pacific whose programs, at least in connection with the new idea, were on paper only. Opposition stemmed not only from fear that the Cascade program would be compromised, if not lost, but also from belief that the new venture would be found to be illegal in the end.

D R. BULGIN and Dr. Gaspers prepared a proposal for the training of high school teachers for the state of Oregon. The tentative plan was produced by them and submitted by June 1, 1965. Both men went their way, each back to his contract obligations, but Bulgin was to return as the Provost of the Associated Christian Colleges of Oregon.

As of September 1, Dr. Bulgin opened up his offices in Tigard. The overall umbrella under which he worked was to bring together a new school of education — acceptable to Salem and at the same time acceptable to the three boards of trustees, three presidents, three deans, three directors of teaching programs, three education faculties, and three combinations of other faculty involved in teaching subject matter norms. ACCO itself would graduate these candidates. Faculty committees were appointed to represent all three schools, meeting for the first time at Cannon Beach in a common workshop. This group worked for nine months on the proposed structure of ACCO—faculty configuration, teaching norms, logistics.

Then the bomb burst. The State Department reversed all previous directives: ACCO itself could not grant degrees or be authorized to set up the program. Actually, it could not be thought of as a true educational institution. Accreditation could only be granted to a college, and ACCO was not a college. Dr. Bulgin gloomily reported his findings and made the trip to Salem. Yes, what he had feared was indeed the truth. The work of months, both his own and that of Dr. Gaspers, based as it was on the directives given out by the offices in the State Department, was all for naught.

Left completely in disarray, there was nothing to do except return to an earlier stance in which ACCO would be the servant of the three schools, simply providing the structure for cooperation. It was our original concept and probably closer to what members of the Higher Commission envisioned; the problem again centered around the irresponsibility and callousness of a bureaucracy sending down mandates which kept us and our associates spinning our wheels for months at a time. Dr. Bulgin devoted many hours of work to developing a new position, calling upon expertise of the ACCO governors, the respective boards of trustees, the deans, and their faculties. Probably, a year or more was taken up in the adjustment—a very precious year in George Fox history.

OUT OF ALL THIS, we took counsel from our education people, specifically Dr. Moore and Professor Paul Cammack working in cooperation with Dr. Bulgin, who recommended several significant actions: (1) improve our educational library, (2) choose our teaching norms, (3) engage clinical professors necessary to handle those norms, and (4) designate a full-time director of teacher training, something which we had never been able to justify in the past.

Improvements to the educational library were effected through Hill Foundation grants, which is explained in great detail elsewhere. A teaching norm, in the Oregon sense, is a concentration of studies in a given content field sufficient to equip a candidate to teach that field at the high school level. In most instances, it is equivalent to a strong minor, differing from a major or minor not only in total hours, but in the provision made to actually teach it under supervision. Generally speaking, a small college will not endeavor to set up norms in every field, but only where justified by exceptional teaching strength, library resources, equipment and buildings, or perhaps when the field is especially close to the tradition of the college. We settled on English literature, physical education, Spanish, music education, biology, and history.

The third recommendation stems from the acceptance in Oregon of the concepts enunciated by Dr. James Conant in his book, *The Education of American Teachers,* in which he popularized the term "clinical professor." The idea comes out of the practice in medical training, adding deeper significance to the practice teaching experience. Practice teaching put the burden on the "master" teacher under whom the candidate spent time in the classroom. The Conant concept puts more responsibility onto the college offering the degree. Each teaching norm must be accompanied by a clinical professor: someone who displays an aptitude in adapting the subject matter to the high school mind, keeps in touch with high school developments, spends time in the classroom setting. Although the Conant idea was most excellent, its implications posed new challenges to the dean and division chairs in hiring for new positions.

The fourth, calling for a full-time director of teacher training, in one sense ought to have preceded all the others. Ideally, this person could then build up the library, be involved in selecting the norms, and in candidating for clinical professors. But time could not await the ideal—too much had been lost already. At any rate, all of these important and necessary developments could come along, one after another or all at once. To the credit of our Board of Trustees, I never noted a moment's hesitation.

THE PERIOD OF 1965 to 1967 was as difficult a time as we have experienced in trying to justify any expenditure, any additional personnel, or any new move. But the research of Dr. Bulgin was so candid and forthright and the claims of Salem so arbitrary that nothing else could be done. Number four came to be our next step. Here again, the idea of trying to find the best was put into play — we developed a master list of candidates, then we went after them.

In the fall of 1966, we contracted one of the finest young scholars in the field, Dr. David Myton, formerly of Ohio. A Friends minister, he graduated from Cleveland Bible College and Youngstown University. His master's in education was from the University of Pittsburgh, his doctorate from Ohio State University in Columbus. He was immediately thrown into the final stages of our self-study.

Progress had been made in terms of actually getting onto the state calendar looking toward accreditation. In the spring and early summer of 1966, most of the material for the self-study was amassed and collated. We discovered that the requirements of the state were more technical and comprehensive than the accreditation procedures of the Northwest Association. We did not have adequate personnel and found it challenging to get everything completed for a Labor Day deadline. With everyone pulling together and people such as Dr. Moore and Dr. Myton working into the wee small hours, it was submitted to Salem the day after Labor Day. It was a most excellent document, and will certainly stand as the best ever produced by our people up to that date. We had many compliments from the State Department and members of the visiting committee.

An Oregon State visiting committee is a pretty impressive aggregation. This one totaled seventeen! The temperaments of these people seemed to be ideally suited to come to our college. They seemed to have the attitude, "We are here to help." When it came time for the general meeting to review their recommendations, it was a truly satisfying one. They made many worthwhile and reasonable suggestions. But, even more gratifying was the thread of sincere compliments running throughout. We heard such things as "A much stronger college than I imagined," "Today I heard the best classroom teaching I have ever heard," or "The developments here are truly amazing."

The written reports which were turned in to the State Department only reinforced the oral statements. With the written report, we were told by the State Department to go into the year 1967-68 implementing the suggestions, operating a full program, preparing for the second (and hopefully final) review. No exact date was named, however.

LET US NOW go back and bring up to date our dealings with the Higher Commission in our overall institutional accreditation. In 1964 after the review by the committee led by Father Leary, correspondence was later received indicating that George Fox could look toward a full three years of approval. We assumed a full self-study and visit would occur near the end of the three-year period.

I knew that a full self-study took upwards of a year's time and I was concerned lest an oversight would put us in jeopardy, so I asked what George Fox could expect. I was told not to be concerned — another full self-study would not be required! The significance of this news could hardly be fathomed at first. The pressure was off! The sentiment of the Higher Commission was strong enough to spare us the work and cost of constant self-studies. It was assumed that no calamity could now befall us such as an abrupt withdrawal of accreditation.

Dr. Bemis, a member of the committee, came to evaluate us in May, 1967, thereafter reporting to the summer meeting of the Higher Commission. His visit was altogether cordial and satisfactory; he recommended continued full status to the Higher Commission, who heartily concurred, and when the Association met the last of November, it also unanimously voted our continued regional accreditation for another three years.

We knew that we were not yet in the class of strong colleges or universities who were granted status for up to eight or ten years, but it was highly significant that we would not be asked to undergo an evaluation for at least six years. The sixties proved to be different in so many ways from the forties and early fifties—the little Quaker college was on its way; it was a genuine college which could be a source of pride to its alumni and friends, and worthy of the extended support of the church and the coporate world.

The "mechanics" of administration and finance—the "bread and butter" day to day operations—compose the subject matter of the following chapter.

Chapter four

Administration and Finance

"**D**ID YOUR EXPERIENCES as a Friends pastor stand you in good stead when you became a college president?" It was D. Clyde Milner, the president of Guilford College in North Carolina, who, taking me by the arm at the annual meeting of the Quaker college presidents, was becoming acquainted with the freshman member of the team from Oregon. Until that time, only eighteen months after being elected, I had not been able to comprehend all the differences in the two callings, but he had put his finger on one of them! I had to answer, "No, they have not."

Unless one is a student of Friends history, the significance of the conversation may not mean too much. But to one coming up through the ranks of the ministry, then being initiated into the fairly exclusive Quaker college group numbering only ten other members, the question had a pointed relevance. The role of Quaker ministry has been clamped into certain rigid patterns in different countries and different centuries. True, George Fox, the English reformer and founder, called forth his "Valiant Sixty." Some were highly educated with years at Oxford University or the Sorbonne behind them. Others were tradesmen. Still others were stripling youths not old enough to have had a trade, but all answering the call to preach the liberating gospel of the Lord Jesus Christ. Fox himself relegated formal education to a secondary role in favor of the primary anointing of the Holy Spirit, claiming that "neither

Cambridge nor Oxford makes the preacher." While the first generation "liberated" men and women to preach, there followed one
hundred and fifty years of quiet with comparatively little formal
education or formal activity. It was not until after the Civil War
that the revivalist movement shook American Quakers out of their
lethargy in the second half of the nineteenth century. The role of
pastoral leadership slowly became formally recognized and only
in certain parts of the world. Thousands of Friends still attended
meetings without pastoral leadership. Until then, government of
meetings had been divided among clerks and elders and overseers
with every member having a voice in the meeting. The new pastoral relationship at first demanded no change in the discipline at
all; rather, one of the resident ministers was chosen to preach more
often than others, and the fellowship promised to take on some
farming or other business, releasing the minister to give more time
to pastoral calling.

Evolution into the pastoral system was not intended to bring
about a new professional class. Elders and overseers still held the
"top" positions, many times for life. I can remember in my early
pastoral experience that elders and overseers in meetings where I
served still conceived of pastors as coming and going while they
(the elders and overseers) continued in their positions for life.

Serious claim was given honestly and honorably to the fact
that God himself ordained a person to the Christian ministry. There
was no doubt about, it. Appeals were made for youth to give themselves to the work at home and abroad. These were high and holy
tasks. But a thoughtful and candid appraisal of the position of the
Friends church during its period of embracing the pastoral system
must admit to several inconsistencies and "blind spots." One was
in the relatively low provision for salaries. Another allowed that
little or no schooling was essential. For instance, I recall that when
I was recorded a minister in Oregon Yearly Meeting in 1934, there
was only one other pastor then serving a church who was a college
graduate.

But for my purpose here, the major problem stemmed from the relatively "fuzzy" position of the pastor in regard to the leadership of the meeting. On one hand, a pastor was looked up to as especially called of God while on the other hand addressed simply by first and last name; as often as not worked at an outside occupation as any other member of the meeting; and deferred to the wisdom and spiritual insight of other ministers, elders, and overseers — neither higher nor lower in leadership. The Society and the meeting were greater and more lasting than any one person, perhaps for many generations before and long after the individual had been forgotten. Churches did not come and go nor did cults grow up around the personality of any one pastor. For a generation or two after transition, the pastor could find little in writing concerning the position. Confidence and love granted acceptance which no amount of "job description" could supply. The pastor was encouraged to preach, pray, and call on people. Any kind of "program" or strategy for outreach or growth was unknown. Involvement in business of the meeting was minimal; I have known fellow pastors as late as 1940 who seldom if ever spoke in the monthly business meeting. Only within recent years have pastors come forward with programs outlining the work of the church in all its phases for a year at a time. Counseling services, community outreach, family togetherness emphases, paid choir leaders, would all be for a later day. Pastors did not do anything unilaterally — service was accomplished within the community of believers.

How different this is from the administrative function of a college president! On my first day behind the desk, I was besieged with a volley of questions from faculty and students, all of whom demanded immediate answers. Decision-making had never been considered or discussed in any ministers' conference I had ever attended!

THE FIRST REQUEST I put before the Board of Trustees on the very evening of my election was that they appoint an Administrative Committee both for my protection and my assistance. The committee of five (myself, the vice president and three deans) has been "The Administration" for all of the years since. Meeting weekly, minutes have been kept since 1965. A line of succession has been built into the organization with a revolving second and third position, so that at all times the college has the security of a chief officer in charge on campus, the organization functioning in the absence of the president. It has not broken down in all these years. There is unanimity in most decisions, but if there is a minority opinion, it is noted and recognized. If there is honest dissent, we defer to the specialty of the person involved. In light of this administrative structure, responsible action at the time is not reversed upon the president's return to campus. I do not "crack knuckles."

There are several effects of this method. People left in charge behave in a free and responsible manner. Action is taken when it should be taken. Junior officers "blossom" in the sunlight of confidence. Incidentally, there is not a great backlog of messy detail or crises hanging over my return, and only the most difficult or complex situations are held for my personal review. This is not to say that mistakes, even grievous errors, have not been made. But at the moment we stand together, maintaining a front of unity and responsible action. Later, if the position is found to be untenable, or subsequent intelligence changes our perspective, we may alter our stand agreeably.

A president must act promptly and fairly. A college cannot operate in a vacuum. My early months in office must have been a trial to others along these lines, as well as to myself. I had very little administrative background. In over twenty years of pastoral experience, I had never had my own church office, let alone a secretary; at over forty years of age, I had never dictated a letter! What little filing I had done was my biblical subject matter and sermons, and was incomplete and haphazard to say the least. I had little penchant for detail. I was given to snap judgment, often biased by a lack of full or balanced information. Going to my office each day as early as possible I had my devotional quiet time, asking God for wisdom—especially that we should all be protected from error, mistakes in judgment, and scandal which could bring disrepute to his name and the college in particular. As difficult decisions had to be made, they were often wiser and more equitable than my human wisdom alone could have dictated. I fell into a manner of asking for time while I reviewed all sides of a problem. This was especially necessary coming into a professional situation without the benefit of much administrative history, let alone college or educational administrative history. I would request of the person asking for a decision time to look into different facets, interview others likely to be affected, ascertain if there were regulations or methods which already addressed the subject, or make a judgment based upon a body of precedent already established. The Administrative Committee was consulted. Then, and only then, could there be a second interview at an agreed upon time. The method thus outlined stood the test as novel situations presented themselves until I was able to rely upon a greater habitual experience strengthened by acceptance.

WHILE I AM addressing myself to the subject of decision making, I give credit to other persons who have contributed to a better administration at George Fox. I think of Dr. Frank Griffin, interim president at Reed College, and Dr. Morgan Odell at Lewis and Clark, who served their respective institutions during my early months. Both President Harry Dillin of Linfield College and Dr. Herbert Smith of Willamette University (my alma mater) provided invaluable knowledge of finance and development. Dr. Seth Eastvold of Pacific Lutheran helped me greatly in church relations. Dr. Tom Jones, just finishing his illustrious career at Earlham, was a tower of strength, taking a personal interest in me and giving me confidence and encouragement when I saw little hope. During this time I came to know more intimately the men in leadership in the other Friends schools, and their battles and successes gave me a wealth of information which could be adapted easily into the

George Fox situation: Dr. Byron Osborne and Dr. Everett Cattell in their dramatic transition from Cleveland Bible College to Malone College in Canton, Ohio; Dr. Samuel Marble at Wilmington with student development and employment programs; Dr. Clyde Milner at Guilford regarding adult housing; Dr. Paul Smith of Whittier and the dormitory financing he was able to effect; President Charles A. Ball and his successful community relations at William Penn; and Dr. Courtney Smith and Swarthmore's simply marvelous publications. Perhaps, almost by osmosis, a person picks up "know-how" from those who are more knowledgeable and who have had experiences which they are willing to share.

I have made it a practice to get to all of the conferences and workshops possible, especially if they were funded or could be grouped together with other trips and obligations. Beginning with the first meeting of CASC in 1956 and my election to that board, I attended all of the scheduled meetings for five years, averaging four a year. I coupled these with the annual conventions of the Quaker college presidents. Also being elected to the board of the Christian Freedom Foundation, I attended all of its meetings in New York City. But I highlight three conferences which stand out as especially significant in my own experience and which added to the success and prestige of George Fox as an institution.

The first of these was the annual meeting of the Northwest Association for Higher Education held in 1958 at Southern Oregon College in Ashland. The main subject was "Honors Programs," featuring Dr. Joseph Cohen of Colorado State University, and out of the program and discussions our own Intensified Studies program was born.

The second was our invitation to participate in the western section of the celebrated Intellectual Life Conferences at Wagon Wheel Gap, Colorado. It was, without doubt, the greatest mental stimulus that I had ever experienced up to that time. I was mentally hungry, and although I am never satisfied, I ate the most satisfactory meal in all my life to date. I experienced a spiritual as well as intellectual blessing for in the words of Louis Benezet as he closed the sessions: "A Greater than Plato was here."

The third was my opportunity to enroll in the Graduate School of College Administration at the University of Michigan under the tutelage of Dr. Algo T. Henderson. Concepts of job description, administrative structures, authority, decision making, delegation, et cetera, learned there have been put in practice ever since.

These all are illustrative of the great debt I owe to those who have been my mentors, to all the opportunities of friendship, counsel, and sharing which have given me insights to better accomplish my tasks, and to all of the broadening experiences in reading and travel which I have been able to exploit. All have become a part of the history being spun out in these pages.

ON MY DESK the first day as president, Dean McNichols had placed a copy of the Faculty Handbook prepared by Dr. Paul Parker as part of his application data to the Higher Commission. It numbered six or seven pages setting forth a page of professional ethics, a statement of Christian educational policy, and a list of committees. The Dean felt that a more detailed statement of educational aims and goals should be included which had been passed by the board in the winter of 1953-54.

From these simple and humble beginnings, the Faculty Handbook (later to become the Administrative and Faculty Handbook) evolved to embrace the operational structure. A study of the handbook will show the growth of complexity. It grew in two ways: first, as practices evolved, it would appear advantageous to officially adopt the methods which were proving successful. The faculty and/or the administration, would prepare the sense and wording for the concurrence of the board. Second, new needs or directions were anticipated and a written policy drafted in advance. As often as not, these changes came about at the same time as amendments were made to the constitution and bylaws.

Leaves and sabbaticals illustrate how the first type and the second type often merged. The older edition of the handbook contained no sabbatical policy, simply because the college never boasted one — there had never been money to pay for work which was not being done! Of course, this situation could not be countenanced forever. The needs of three professors brought it to a head. Professor Paul Mills, after years of faithful service, had a great longing to see and study in the Holy Land. He had planned and saved, but circumstances had previously prevented him from going. One of the grants from the Calder Foundation was for faculty fringe benefits, and we allowed him $2,000. Obviously that amount would not cover all the expenses for serious study in Israel and Jordan, but he added funds of his own, and not only visited Palestine but went all the way around the world, becoming acquainted with our alumni on mission fields.

When Dr. Arthur Roberts asked for time away for writing and respite, the Academic Affairs Committee of the board championed the idea, although there was no money for a replacement. Due to a misunderstanding with the full board, we realized we needed to work responsibly within a framework of minuted action and a written policy.

At the same time, the satisfactory policy which allowed full-time faculty to attend summer school on salary was strained when Sheldon Louthan wished to continue from the summer into the fall term at the University of Oregon. There followed almost two years when we tried desperately to secure funds through an estate, and later through more liberal federal programs. All of these men were tenured and embodied the commitment and leadership that we wished to secure and hold, but they needed financial support to complete their doctoral studies.

Professor Harvey M. Campbell, during his stint as Dean of Administration, did an excellent job creating the administrative chart which brought unity to the structure and better descriptions of the duties of officers and committee members. Dean Cole, with the concurrence of Dr. Moore, separated the administration and its committees from faculty appointments while the professional status of the clerical, maintenance, and custodial staffs was defined and elucidated. Finally, the work of Sheldon Louthan and Thomas Sine, Dean of Students, clarified rules and standards of student conduct, and ways the student body was included with the faculty and administration on certain dual committees affecting their areas of interest.

MAY I TAKE US now along tree-lined paths, past formal plazas, and into gardens where the birds sing in the springtime? The area of campus development and beautification may have not all been as idyllic as my opening sentence suggests. All the same, early on I found the possibilities greatly to my liking, and as my family certifies, I have given countless hours to this happy avocation. Trying to analyze the reasons for my involvement, I have come up with a number of things which will not only throw light upon a necessary aspect of college administration, but may illumine my own interests and personality.

The campus of Pacific and George Fox was basically beautiful and ideal for a small liberal arts college. It had grown to thirty-six acres by the time this narrative begins. History may show that it was not large enough for all of the needs of the future. Most of the buildings were located in a sector at the southwest corner instead of radiating from the center of the campus, although this was not seen as a limitation at the time. It lay in two major sections—the west end with buildings, drives, sidewalks, parking, and foliage trees, and the larger eastern portion, still the "forest primeval." The canyon, majestic with mighty firs, cottonwoods, spruces, and cedars, lovely in the fall with flaming vine maple and golden oaks, was at the same time, an unkempt jungle of hazelnuts, blackberries, and poison oak! Once there had been a bridge spanning Hess Creek but the bridge had broken down and been removed long since. At one time, President Pennington had had an architect prepare plans depicting an impounded lake with canoeists lazing on its surface. I have seen the picture. It was a grand idea, and maybe in the future his dream can yet be realized. The plan showed room for a full quarter-mile track and an amphitheater capable of seating 2,000 spectators. This area would also give place to modern buildings for a resident campus, echoing to the fun and laughter of students, the thunder of football games, the lilt of aspiring vocalists, and budding instrumentalists.

All of this began to grow on me. I tramped in sunshine and rain over every foot of our property. I stepped off distances. I compared one vista with another, I surveyed in my mind for halls and streets and plantings. After the death of my wife, Helen, I found great solace in hours of recollection and imagination. Two factors played into my hand the first year. One was that during the late forties when professor Howard Royle taught biology, a botanical map had been prepared showing the trees and major shrubbery, replete with their coded botanical names. This fine map hung in my outer office. The other was that two conscientious objectors, John Davies and J. D. Baker, were doing their alternative service in 1953-54, being assigned to campus work. They removed a border of Oregon broadleaf maples from the parking strip on Meridian Street, while a later crew would eventually do the same to a similar objectionable planting along the south side of the square adjoining Sheridan Street.

These two factors—the map showing the present plantings and the work already started on taking care of problems and difficulties—coming together in the first days of my presidency were prophetic of what needed to be done. Little by little, plans took shape.

John Davies, quietly interested and loving every tree and bush, came forward with clear, workable ideas about improving the landscape. Later, he invested portions of his own money to buy trees which he and I agreed upon. Howard Harmon of Tacoma, who as a Friends patron of the college, and director of the famous Point Defiance Park, had access to extra shrubbery. He became increasingly interested and following the spring of 1954, sent down several trailer loads of shrubbery, primarily rhododendrons and camellias, which eventually became very substantial and lovely indeed.

Out of my trampings and discussions and trips and musings, the fact emerged that while the campus was dramatically beautiful at a distance with its great oaks, Ponderosa pines, and native firs, up close there were few, if any, foundation plantings. Most of the concrete or board foundations used to move buildings came out of the ground naked and bare, only to be stained with the ever-present Oregon winter mud. In the words of an eminent American artist, "there was not enough to arrest the eye." There was barrenness and drabness. What plantings there were looked scabby and unkempt and unpruned. Many trees boasted rotten limbs. Trees coming up haphazardly as sprouts, grew merrily toward heaven without an overall master plan.

One never knows when student sentiment may bring to light a glaring need. I was interviewed by a delegation made up mostly of seniors, who had been considering the nature and cost of their gift to the college when they graduated. Among others, they had seen a need for park benches. Said one, "President Ross, there is no place on the campus to sit down." Sure enough, there were shady spots and green grass, nooks and woodsy paths, but not a settee or a stone rest anywhere to be seen.

The first seats built to rectify the omission were those of brick and concrete installed with our own hands where Hoover Hall had been. Now for the first time a student could sit comfortably to study out of doors, or talk with friends. Now there are many such places, some of brick, others of impervious redwood.

Although it was difficult to imagine it at the time, the more developed area of campus to the west (surrounding Wood-Mar Hall) and the canyon (primitive area), which were almost completely separate, were to become one and the same as the improved section grew. The canyon area contained some giant old-growth firs and hemlocks. Over the years since the days of the pioneers, some selective logging had been done, either for thinning or to take care of trees fallen from winter storms. In either case, the result was cord wood for hungry furnaces. Wood-Mar was heated with wood clear up until 1964. Great ricks of cord wood gracing the campus are a nostalgic memory for most of the alumni.

If we were to expand, if we were to clean up the place, the heavy forest must be reduced to a park, old stumps removed, and rotten fells bulldozed and burned. The first selections for cutting were made by Wayne Roberts, Yamhill county agent, who was later assisted by forestry experts from the Protective Association headquarters at Forest Grove. Different outfits made agreements with us: two large contracts went to sawmills, with the college getting a share; one cutting of cottonwoods went for excelsior on which we made a good profit; other smaller and knottier trees were used for our own furnaces or sold. There were giant bonfires and prodigious movements of earth from time to time. Architect Don Lindgren supervised all the work in order to protect the future beauty of the campus. Over the next five or six years of major cutting and cleanup the entire eastern horizon opened up, giving us lovely new vistas, the best trees artistically placed with room for proposed buildings, drives, and domestic plantings.

BUT THERE WERE catastrophes, as well, which marred our hopes and plans. One occurred when the infamous Columbus Day storm hit on the evening of October 12, 1962. Nothing like it had ever occurred in the Northwest. Winds up to 127 mph hurled themselves in from the Pacific, from south to north, and for some three hours wreaked havoc all the way from Coos Bay to Vancouver, B.C. I was out in it the entire time, trying to keep our student body under control and generally protect the buildings and grounds, but I was helpless and knew it—only it was so thrilling, why go inside? Tree limbs the size of a person's thigh sailed by like horizontal projectiles. One of the handsome Ponderosa pines, a full four-feet thick, snapped off like a match stick. The great firs, fifty, sixty, even seventy feet high, bowed in the force until their tops touched the ground—some to be snapped off or uprooted, others to painfully right themselves. The immediate loss was substantial, although not as much as we feared. Most of the buildings were intact with the exception of a temporary roof on the Minthorn remodeling job. But forty of our trees were gone! Some of the finest of them were so badly mangled or uprooted that they had to be destroyed. The tall, stately hemlock, just to the south of the tennis courts, went over, destroying itself as well as smashing the steel fence. It took months of laborious clean up and the scars still remain. As bad as anything, though, has been the creeping death—still with us—as so many giants and lesser trees weakened by twisting and broken roots, unknown at first, have succumbed. Not only did we suffer an irreparable loss in value and beauty, our challenges of landscaping were multiplied, and it will be a generation or more before we get back to where we were before that storm.

The major project, or series of them, however, was moving forward with an ongoing program of beautification beginning with foundation plantings and later the formation of complete landscaping plans under the supervision of professionals. During the early years, we were forced to do all we could with very little, accomplishing what needed to be done with donated plants, time, and money. As I have said, friends began to come forward with bushes, trees, cuttings, seeds, and roots. Growing up as I had in the lush Willamette Valley, I knew there were landscape nurseries everywhere, many of them large commercial enterprises, nation-wide in advertising and reputation. I prepared a letter asking for donations, promising to provide a tax deductible receipt proving the gift in kind and the value to a nonprofit benevolent corporation. The response was tremendous! First one and then another donated truckloads of shrubbery. Some stock was large and misshapen and had to be dug by our own crew. Some had to be picked up, but some was already balled and delivered to campus. Big plants which did not have a ready sale to the average weekend gardener were ideal for the college with its large buildings and broad, grassy lawns. Our figures showed at least $2,500 wholesale value was donated in the first twelve months. Several firms donated to George Fox annually thereafter when they cleaned up sections of their nurseries or closed out sales yards. Not only did we plant hundreds of nice bushes and trees, we also maintained a heeling-in nursery of our own west of the gymnasium until the winter of 1966-67. There we kept a revolving supply of stock not yet needed, ones too small for planting, or misshapen trees and shrubs awaiting the pruning knife and balance that only time and nature can lend.

Time fails to give credit to all, but I think of Henry Church who was heart broken when the county decided to eliminate a lovely redwood which he and his wife had bought years before as a little burl on their honeymoon. It took a good deal of ingenuity, a wrecking truck, and eventually a big bladed bulldozer, but that imposing giant is now a part of the campus, standing to the west of Calder Center.

Stuart Richey, director of maintenance, approached me on behalf of his friend, M. Cecil Smith, a horticulturist par excellence, who wished to thin out his prizewinning rhododendrons. Cecil showed us his acres of exotic plants, pointing out those marked for removal and explaining each variety's growth patterns and order of blossom, especially if their habitat required full or partial shade or allowed full sunshine. These were all large and robust plants of excellent quality. Some were quite rare. Later, when the season was right, our crews worked with him, bringing over two heavy truckloads of exquisite shrubbery which now grace our campus.

Friends and patrons gave us overgrown or surplus shrubbery. Others brought native plants and small trees. Joan Dunkel, the first of the fine professors who signed on in 1954, used her enthusiasm to have her students label the trees of the main campus with their correct botanical names. The men's garden club asked for a project and provided all of the camellias and azaleas on the circle drive—plowing, mulching, fertilizing, lifting, and planting. Some plantings were cut in half; some had grown too big in their former location. Some, such as the traditional Senior Rose Garden, now being in the shade north of Wood-Mar Hall, had to be transplanted out in the sun. Some were moved three or four times. We used students on cleanup days prior to Homecoming and May Day, and they enjoyed actual planting more than the busywork of simply raking leaves. Alice and I marked one vine maple in the canyon, bringing it out when dormant and planting to advantage in the sunken garden of the Student Union. Although the transformation could not be noticed significantly from any one season to the next, the cumulative change has been dramatic.

When we first got into the building programs, we still "robbed" from established plantings to provide for new buildings. We did so with the Student Union, and even for Shambaugh Library and Pennington Hall, we were thinking small. We put lawn and parking, but no shrubbery, in the contract so we had to add landscaping gradually to complete the projects. Even now some buildings have little or no shrubbery. "Never again," decided Don Lindgren. All later buildings had landscaping in the contract and had their shrubbery installed by the time of dedication. Over the years, first by hard work, imagination, and little actual money, and later by professional contracting, our campus has changed much to the better.

AND NOW, I introduce the very important subject of our endowment. A brief comment may be remembered from the allusion to accrediting in chapter 3, but the history of its growth merits ample space in its own right.

Philosophically early leaders of the college knew that an invested endowment was ideal and necessary. At the same time, endowment funds for any college are hard to come by, and I hazard that no college or university will admit to having enough. Some very substantial schools find themselves with relatively small endowments, and will without doubt suffer because of the lack. It is said that in 1904 Mr. Mills, a Friend who owned land east of the college church (the first site of the Academy built in 1885), sold his holdings there and the fund was used to initiate the endowment.

A detailed study shows some modest additions to the fund, but the construction of Wood-Mar Hall sapped the college supporters, and World War I was a difficult time for Quakers. It took the drives of the 1920s to provide a sizeable amount as Dr. Levi Pennington notes in his book entitled, *Rambling Recollections of Ninety Happy Years*. His ingenuity and the stewardship of Friends created an endowment which has been a strength to Pacific and George Fox ever since. Much of the total came to be invested in Yamhill County real estate, which after the demand for dried Italian prunes fell off and the Great Depression hit, dropped alarmingly. But so did gilt-edged stocks and bonds of all kinds, and the investments, shepherded wisely, saved the college. It is said that Pacific College came through better than any other Oregon school.

Frank C. Colcord was a remarkable man, trustee and chair of the Investment Committee until his untimely death in August, 1967. A dinner was given in Frank's honor during the winter of 1958 and at that time he had already served his alma mater for twenty-eight years. He had made a career with the Portland General Electric Company, retiring from that career to join the college staff as a "dollar-a-year" man until the day of his death. His great contribution was his work on the investment portfolio of Pacific and George Fox. He became highly skilled and recognized in financial circles.

There are several notable characteristics of the portfolio which should be recognized. One is that there has never been a taint of scandal occasioned by misappropriation. In keeping with Quaker testimony, conscientious control of the investments is maintained by avoiding investment in military industries, liquor production, and tobacco manufacture and sale. These are complicated issues and difficult because of united funds, great cartels and diversified corporations, but a serious and successful attempt to maintain our witness has been the policy of the committee over the years. Frank made it the aim of his life to boost the endowment to one million dollars. At the audit in June, 1967, just before his death, it stood at $1,220,000.

Recent programs have brought some growth. We have made it a policy to use one-half of any estate over $1,000, not earmarked otherwise, for the endowment. Another policy has been to include an amount for the endowment whenever a building is financed. This plan has not always been successful, although $20,000 was added at the time of the drive for Shambaugh Library and some annuities have been assigned to endowment. All buildings should be secured by endowment for their maintenance and replacement — there is no argument to the theory, but it has been our unhappy experience that gifts for brick and mortar, equipment, books, and visible needs come far more readily than for hidden investments from which only the income can be used each year. With the inflationary spiral of modern conditions and the increasing needs of higher education, we would need to add at least one million dollars a year to our principal to stay even, let alone improve our relative position.

The ratio of endowment income to total annual needs shrinks each year. Our situation at George Fox is far from unique, but that does not make it any easier. A glance at our records will reveal that in 1953-54 our general budget was approximately $92,000, while endowment income was close to $23,000 (25 percent). In 1967-68 the total operating budget came to $811,000, and the endowment, realized $32,000 (4 percent). A popular school of thought, first championed by A. V. Wilker of Union Carbide, is that large investments may not be the best answer to college stability — why not secure annual grants from corporations and foundations? It can be shown that an allocation from a single foundation may be equal to the total income of all the investments laboriously accrued over many years. We can testify to the truth of the new theory. More than once in the last decade, one grant, or two smaller ones, has equaled our total endowment income. I readily admit to the temptation of building budgets on unrealistic expectations! The modern experience, notwithstanding, we fear that foundation grants can prove to be a broken reed, and a board of directors conducting the affairs of a foundation can casually change from one designation to another—adding, reducing, specifying, controlling, limiting. It is too easy to depend upon free, undesignated gifts and build them into budgets. We now know something of the variability of foundation grants: the whims of directors, rulings of the IRS, the provisions of wills, and the popularity of new programs replacing older ones wreak havoc with attempts to stabilize day-to-day operation. One can live with these changes if they can be anticipated and included in the budget forecast, but *havoc* is the only word if they come abruptly in the middle of the year. The greatest difficulty can be experienced if a previously open grant is converted to a special project, thus reducing income to the general budget. All of which brings us to the subject of budgets—the general one in particular.

*I*F EVER there has been a dramatic change in the operation of the business of our college, it is this! The old system was based on simple income and expense. Income came from student tuition and fees, room and board, endowment, and gifts. Disbursements were made for salaries, library, auxiliary enterprises, and maintenance. The trick was to keep the disbursements equal to or less than the income. There were several ways in which it could be accomplished—giving the faculty only what was available, buying less equipment or fewer books, turning off the lights, or letting the paint peel and the grass grow! Sometimes, in dire emergency, the faculty took promissory notes for their salaries.

My first budgeting experience was scarcely more complex. I was given to understand that its creation was primarily up to my guesswork, and so a series of erasures and additions and subtractions must balance on paper. There were a number of fairly constant income items—tuition, room and board, fees, and endowment. Expenses included salaries, taxes, food, light, heat, maintenance. The entire set of figures came to less than a page. I recall my ignorance and innocence. I had only two challenges: raise enough money and hold down expenses!

As we grew, we began creating a variety of designated funds for specific projects—chairs, books, microscopes, a Baldwin organ, sign boards, roofing, trees, draperies, and girls' dormitories. Next, I made the disconcerting discovery that I had inherited a number of prepaid claims. There were estates in which grandchildren were to get free tuition. I found scratch papers indicating parents had made payment years before for their child's schooling. The class of one year had made a contribution for a project never completed. Then I unearthed the same problem with another class. Complications of even greater magnitude arose. Once, an estate needed to be settled after the death of a claimant, and we were forced to come up with $1,000, then another for $5,000, and once even $20,000! We could absorb a year's tuition, but it was another thing altogether to come up with hard cash. We found ourselves absorbing too many expenses and borrowing against the general fund for demands when we had no hope of repayment. We went into a morass, and knew no way to extricate ourselves. In addition to these somber revelations, we came up against two more demands for which we had no reserve. Paving assessments were made by the city on peripheral streets adjacent to the campus, and there was an increase in insurance premiums, in part because we had not carried sufficient coverage and in part because underwriters' inspections revealed unknown dangers.

By 1956, total outstanding obligations came to $144,000. It was too much. It hung around us like a millstone. It was a real threat to the continuance of the college. It was an even greater threat psychologically. We Quakers were guilty of not managing our affairs wisely and living within our income. It was terribly depressing to all of the trustees who were privy to the problem.

I nearly collapsed under it and went out to the Oregon coast for a month-long recluse. While there, Dr. John Brougher invited all of the trustees to come to his lovely home on the Columbia River to consider the debacle. Out of earnest prayer and a spirit of unity and sacrifice, the men took on themselves what later came to be known as The Debt Retirement: to pay for a dead horse? To go back and settle up for years in arrears? To set one house in order for a better future? "Yes, yes, and yes." Denver Headrick and I gave our energies to the drive for the next four years. It was highly successful with pledges finally exceeding $150,000. It was tremendously encouraging to all of us — the trustees, our patrons and alumni, our friends in Newberg, our creditors — sparking interest and goodwill wherever George Fox was known. Without doubt, it became the greatest recovery in all our history.

All of this took place under the old accounting system. We realized that our methods of bookkeeping were not adequate. Our auditing firm primarily served for-profit corporations and did not meet the needs of a nonprofit college. Part-time staff could not keep up with the variety of new funds. Questions failed to find answers. Projections proved to be inaccurate. Fixed expenses were often larger than variable income. Here was one of the great problems of private college financing and budgeting: responsible contracting of professors and administrators, done in the early winter and spring of a particular year must anticipate expenditures beginning in the deficit period of the following summer against income not received until September or October. During this time, the proportion of guaranteed income is very small in contrast to the proportion of expenditures. Our experience at George Fox (similar to the ratio of endowment income) has magnified as the college has grown. There is a point of no return which the board encounters six to eight months ahead of the actual end of the year.

The famous "Sixty College Study" threw light on the problem. At any rate, we could learn if one department was being favored while another was starved. At one junction, we had our creditors prepare a twelve-month forecast based on the first six months' expenditures and found that it proved to be inflated because more bills are paid in October and November than at any other period. The executive committee analyzed comparative data. The finance committee and the executive committee got in the habit of beginning their work about a year in advance.

One of the most helpful improvements was to adapt our book-keeping system to one advocated by Arthur French, the former business manager at Wellesley College and author of the first "Sixty College Study." I learned much of the system directly from French himself. Of course, no bookkeeping system can bring in money or hold down expenses in itself, but the system was ideal for a small college. Over the years, we learned better how to identify items, how to control purchase orders, how to allocate adequate and reasonable budgets—sometimes beginning with faculty input before crafing the budget, and at other times beginning with the projected budget and then refining components in conference with faculty and representatives.

DEAN GILFILLAN had prophesied to me around 1957 that "you will be safe if you can make it until 1960." Instead, our problems increased. We had more difficulties in the early 1960s than ever before—they were bigger and more complicated. We took in far more but also spent more. The spring of 1967 was almost more than the board and administration could deal with. We had had years when the enrollment increased by as much as 27 percent. Then the rate fell to 7 percent. We had financed Shambaugh Library by a hair at the First National Bank, secured by our endowment, with the Shambaughs pledging to pay out in thirty-six months. Dr. Shambaugh passed away the year following the dedication and the projected income of the family was reduced due to fewer sales of Albuquerque real estate. Seven years later the account was still open. Federal loans for new buildings tied up the remainder of our endowment as collateral. We had remodeled Kanyon Hall, hoping for a rally of alumni support which never materialized, leaving us in debt. We had budgets for one-third of the total cost of Calder Center to be borne by the federal government, but we suffered from a series of unfavorable rulings: first the architects' fees were not allowed, then home economics was said to be not "science," and finally the agency made their calculations with a formula of 30 percent, as opposed to 33.3 percent. In the end, we had to go deeper into debt in order to cover our costs. After promising the faculty a raise across the board in 1966-67, we did not have the funds necessary to allow the raise. Then we had to borrow and defer a hoped-for raise in 1967-68 as well.

Discussion and study meetings were called, some for the full board but others for the executive committee only, when we wrestled over where and how to reduce. A feeling of discouragement pervaded. Tempers grew short. Some threatened to resign rather than face public censure or the fear of liability. One of the proposals was to make across-the-board cuts. If the forecasted expenditures were expected to be 10 or 15 percent more than the projected income, we would then cut everything accordingly. But, the more we grappled with the issues, the more we realized the impossibility of such an easy formula. Two overriding considerations made it impossible. The first was the controlling factor of fixed expenses. In other words, there were dozens of items which could not be reduced or changed, however nice it might have been to be able to do so. These included high annual interest on loans and time payments; payments on new buildings; loans from two local banks; interest due patrons who had loaned to us over the years; and newer obligations incurred through the annuity program. We had entered into contract for services for students—food service, cleaning, musical instruments, science equipment, and recurring editions of books. These could not be reduced. Therefore, the variables represented only a portion of the budget, but a very sensitive portion.

The second consideration was the philosophical concept of educational priority. There was a great deal of soul-searching in that this period of difficulty was traumatic in the extreme. First, we were obligated to people—faculty, staff, and students. We did not want to do anything that would jeopardize the career of loyal workers or reduce educational opportunities for students. Answers were not simple. What is essential? What traditional offerings are obsolete or in less demand? Can a major be dropped without reducing overall appeal to students and affect the enrollment? Studies were conducted on foreign languages (especially French), home economics, and intercollegiate athletics (especially football). We tried to ascertain if there was a way ACCO could help us out of our dilemma. Facts indicated that salaries had been reduced appreciably and class size increased. At the same time, we realized that ACCO, for the time being, was a one-way street bilaterally with Cascade: George Fox provided the teachers and Cascade did not pay! In one sense, it may appear simple to draft a philosophical statement to the effect that quality is to be maintained, but of what value is quality if our credit is lost and the college were to be forced to the wall? What about security of careers if no one could expect a legal and binding contract? What about faculty raises and fringe benefits if payroll could not be met? Ideally, some kind of academic priority scale would need to be put in place. It appeared to me that the sensible program for the immediate future included these elements: keep Dean Moore and Dean Cole from great discouragement; endeavor to work in harmony with all concerned, but if I could not secure their wholehearted cooperation, then I would have to issue orders and become authoritarian; and finally announce a policy in which the educational careers of students would not be jeopardized. I would take upon myself the odious task of cutting home economics for a year, eliminating French, reducing the number of out of town games, and forcing large freshman classes to be even larger. These were hard times. No one was happy! But Dr. Moore responded dutifully. The faculty was told "no raise" and they signed up anyway. Patrons secured the salary for Helen Street in home economics, and better yet, negotiations were opened with Linfield College for a full major in that field. Money was found for athletics. We anticipated a larger freshman class but without added class sections. There appeared to be no other way out.

In one sense, this narrative may appear more irresponsible than it really was, for our administrators, specifically Frank Cole and Frank Colcord had worked out an acceptable program with the

United States National Bank which was built upon a deficit budget. We admitted we were facing the problem of controlled growth and building costs, and projected that we would solve this problem by 1968 or 1969 at the latest. As an aside, we all could have had annual budgets in the black if we had only lowered our moral and social standards. History shows that an additional twenty-five students could have helped us meet our financial needs in any one year. But the board and the administration, with our eyes wide open, voted time and again, in full unity, that it was better to finance a debt than to lose our Christian image. Our standards and traditions were to be maintained in the faculty and the student body at all times. However, in the summer of 1966, "tight money" hit us. The bankers reversed their previous decision rather than extend the promised financing; we were told the money, even for the current year, might be withdrawn at the end of any one month. Frank Cole projected that the crisis would hit us by December. I was requested to tell the faculty at its preschool retreat. The two Franks had conference after conference with officers and boards of directors of two banks and with our insurance companies. I will say to the credit of the United States Bank that they did not leave us in the lurch. December came and went, and miraculously we had enough for payroll. January came, and with it a large enrollment. Added federal funds also came, some for student loans and work. February came and went. March was the same, then April came with student tuition income again. The board of First National Bank okayed a total refinancing. We expected funds for the April payroll, but they were tied up in detail. We made the payroll even so. Frank Cole aimed at the settlement of major accounts by May 15, but still no funds. He notified the trustees that we could not meet payroll dated May 31. The funds were released to our account May 31! The college, thanks to the candid, responsible assistance of the two Franks and a modern day patron, found itself in a stronger position than ever in our history.

THE FIRST OF TWO very helpful research projects I had discovered from previous years was completed while Dr. Gervais Carey was president. Dr. Walter Williams, Jr., a professor of education at Florida State University at Tallahassee, and a friend and member of Ohio Yearly Meeting, came out to do a study on George Fox College. It may appear surprising that someone from Florida had to be imported to tell us what we should do. However, as was often the case, it is not so much that something new is said, as who says it, and Dr. Williams did a job for the college and the church that put all concerns on the right track for years to come. The recommendations became a "bible" to the trustees, the subsequent administration, and faculty committees, even in our formal representations to the Higher Commission and in letters to corporations. All of our planning, budgeting, public relations, projections of room and building size, et cetera, were controlled by them. It was as though the former years, with all the success and failure, adequacies and ineptitudes, came into focus at the time of Dr. Williams's visit and were weighed in the balance of his judgment. The later years, with all that they held in portent of future greatness burgeoned out from his meetings with the board. His report became a rallying point, in more ways than one. There had been terrible dissention in the board and the church previously, even to the resignation of President Gulley with strong words before and after. There had been a lengthy period of academic mediocrity. The church leaders had stood to one side—hoping, talking, praying, but without a solid backing in stewardship. The alumni had become disillusioned and embittered. The city of Newberg was embarrassed. But the coming of Williams heralded a new day. Everyone was in agreement that his work and recommendations were truly academically sound. The board, united for the first time in many years, needed a direction to pursue—up! Williams's influence was so great and his personality so winsome that he was asked to assume the presidency.

The second project was, in all actuality a result of and corollary to the first. When the Administrative Committee, composed of Dean

Donald McNichols, Professor Paul Mills, and Harlow Ankeny took over the reigns in 1952, they found that not too much had actually been put into effect. The single accomplishment of the committee was to champion the appointment of a long range planning committee. The professional services of Donald Edmundson, architect, were engaged. The committee was in the midst of its work during the spring and summer of 1954, and I recall very favorable impressions of the first meeting I was invited to attend in October. The results of the work up until that time were presented in the form of a campus plot, the first official one produced since the 1920s. New buildings and streets were sketched in. A projection into the area of the canyon was shown. I was excited and so were all present. Here was something to put our teeth into. Here was visual evidence of purpose. Here was an object soon to be hung on the wall of my office to show to interested Friends, alumni, and prospective donors. It could be included in papers to the Higher Commission. The board endorsed it at its next meeting and in all subsequent projections. It was adapted, changed, and extended, but always taking off from this first one. Needs not yet imagined had to be incorporated later in time. Novel federal programs, not yet foreseen by us, dictated a priority and dimension of things which the 1954 drawing could not envision. But, the 1954 plan had one marvelous concept. Mr. Edmundson had used the expertise of a young member of his staff, John Anundson, late of the University of Birmingham and soon to be attached to the Bureau of Urban Planning at the University of Oregon. He laid out a campus divided into three main sectors — academic, living/social, and athletics. On a much longer scale, our new campus would boast an academic mall where all of the classes, lecture halls, laboratories, and library would be in easy proximity. In fact, the library came to be the focal point. In another section, the student union, all of the dormitories, and the dining hall were to be placed. Far removed were the gymnasium, playing fields, track, and courts. What made the concept appealing and acceptable was that Edmundson and Anundson had embraced the better older buildings. The tripartite campus scheme had been shown to be highly popular on new campuses that had been championed in the 1960s by the educational facilities laboratory. To take Wood-Mar Hall, the science hall, and the new gym, all of which had been put up without any idea of a triple plan, and include them nicely was a work of art, indeed. I am debtor to these excellent plans, the first from Dr. Williams the educator, and the second using the firm of Edmundson, Kennedy, and Koerkendorffer.

THIS INTRODUCES US to my association with the people who have made up the Board of Trustees. They are a wonderful group. As far back as I know, the Board of Trustees, or managers as they are historically known, was composed of fifteen men. By the time I came into the picture, Ivan Adams was the chair. I can think of no one better qualified for the job. A graduate of Portland Bible Institute and later Asbury College in Kentucky, he has been in the auditor's office at the First National Bank of Oregon for many years. He has demonstrated a deep understanding of the challenges facing George Fox. He has a keen appreciation of the role of the Christian liberal arts college in today's world. He has shown himself to be essentially fair. He has been a good anchor for me in challenging my progressiveness, while wholeheartedly supporting every move of advancement. He and I have "clicked," and I have found him to be a true friend and brother. What I write about Ivan could be duplicated for one after another of the board members around the table.

As any student of college affairs knows, the greatest responsibility of a Board of Trustees is the selection of a president. The current board has faced this challenge several times in recent years. When Dr. Gervais Carey was invited to assume the presidency, there was general satisfaction, and I may add relief, for he was highly respected by all who knew him. He was a leading biblical scholar, and a suave gentleman. He was young enough that they anticipated he would serve for ten or fifteen years which would give the school a period of significant growth and success. But his health failed and he became terribly discouraged and depressed. When after only three years in leadership he turned in his resignation, there was little that the board could do but accept.

To the credit of Dr. Carey he had worked endlessly to enhance the position of the college. One of the men he hired was Dr. Paul P. Parker, a biologist, a Friends minister, and an educator who served capably as Dean of the college. When he became president following Dr. Carey, expectations were high again, only to be dashed, for under the strenuous load he carried at the college and in his home (his aged father required constant care) Dr. Parker became very ill, and after only two years the board again found itself looking for a president. Two short-lived presidencies can produce a desperate situation for any school, not to say a little non-accredited one in a small town in Oregon. Rather than make a false move, the group did the best they could do for the time— they created an administrative team of three: Dean Donald McNichols, chair; Paul Mills, Professor of Bible; and Harlow Ankeny, Director of Public Relations. These men took on the full administration of George Fox College on top of their full loads.

I have read the minutes and correspondence of those three years that the board members worked diligently to find a replacement. It is a wonder that these men even maintained their health or sanity, let alone found divine resources and wisdom sufficient to operate the school. After a lengthy and exhaustive presidential search I am honored to have been offered the position and to have been privileged to serve in this capacity.

Traditionally, the trustees met once in the fall at Homecoming and again in the spring on May Day. Of course there was an Executive Committee which met often, and the entire board could be called at any time. Part of the legal structure was "the corporation." According to the charter, the corporation was, as its name signified, the true legal entity. Its main duty, in actual practice, was to approve the names of new trustees. Members of the corporation were elected by Oregon Yearly Meeting in session, in five classes of ten persons each. One of the interesting sidelights of the loose and casual operations over some of its past was the great ease in which some aged persons were elected with their name never coming up again for discussion or reappointment. That problem had been addressed during the presidency of Emmett Gully, and in the late 1940s and early 1950s the system was working well enough. There still remained the nagging question if the dual system was really necessary; why call fifty people together for one evening, especially when they had no orientation and little contact with the college during the year, and for such limited purposes? Coupled with this question was another one: how to strengthen the board itself?

*W*HEN I SPEAK of "strengthening" I do not refer to faithfulness or loyalty. Given the number and complexity of problems we faced, we needed more than fifteen board members to add judgment and wisdom: persons from different walks of life; more professionals strategically situated in different parts of the country in order to give visibility; more alumni and church leaders. I did not like the timing of the meetings which denied us the opportunity of attendance at ball games, concerts, plays, and banquets. Some of us were deeply concerned about a stronger official connection with the church. What was needed was a total revamping of the board and its structure, its meetings, and its legal form. Any serious changes would mean a review by yearly meeting in session, and organized change would mean a two-year wait. Nevertheless, the need seemed to dictate a drastic change, however detailed and cumbersome. After due deliberation and with the assistance of our attorney, we drafted a constitution and bylaws which were superior to any previous document.

In addition to other revisions, the number of board members was increased from fifteen to thirty. I proposed a general letter which was sent to prospective candidates to discover if any were willing, if elected, to serve the college given the number and gravity of issues which needed immediate attention. The response was amazing and altogether gratifying. Most were courteous enough to answer and of those, most answered in the affirmative. All of us were overjoyed at the discovery of the great well of goodwill and the desire to serve. A round of interviewing followed in the next months. As the record shows, this was the time we added the Honorable Mark O. Hatfield, the governor of the state of Oregon; Phil Martin and Arnold Owen of California; Glenn Koch of Idaho; Mrs. Shambaugh of Albuquerque, and all the rest.

There were to be two meetings a year: one on the first Saturday in June (commencement time), and another on the first weekend in December. The Executive Committee was enlarged and given the authority to act for the full board in interim. The board itself was the corporation. Step by step the pieces fell into place. The added strength was apparent immediately. It was good to hear new voices when discussions grew intense. Attendance proved to be remarkably strong and meetings were used as times when committees met. Every meeting was opened with prayer while the major ones began with a devotional message prepared ahead by one of the members.

It would be less than truthful to claim that all the meetings accomplished all that we set out to do. Many sessions ran out of time. Preparation of the committees was uneven and sometimes the recommendations and results likewise. Much of the value of general meetings was the light they shed on matters at hand, presentation of talks and papers, new ideas that were generated.

Along with monthly reports, I instituted a sheet entitled "Recommendations and Suggestions" which was distributed in advance of each meeting. Its purpose was to direct our thinking onto the same subjects. Reports were used to make sure that unfinished business was not allowed to remain in an unfinished state. We developed over a period of time, a kind of quick efficiency among the chair, the secretary, and myself, with possible solutions and statements prepared in advance.

TRUSTEES WERE particularly instrumental in discovering and recommending possible candidates in our search for new personnel. Dean Gregory made a trip to New England to talk with

Dr. Arthur O. Roberts and years later put me on the track of Dr. Myron Goldsmith. Gerald Dillon was most helpful in working to get Sheldon Louthan and Dennis Hagen. Ronald Owen recommended Dr. Elver Voth. Ivan Adams suggested names for clinical professors and Dr. Hester pointed me to Frank Colcord. Dr. Wayne Roberts opened up our first interviews with Dr. John Brewster, Dr. Eugene Coffin, and Kenneth Williams. This kind of thing is like the tip of an iceberg. These trustees have in turn positively influenced countless youth who have been challenged to excellence in their chosen professions.

One hears at conferences that trustees should be used in fund-raising. But how? The response to this challenge and obligation of trusteeship is as varied as each personality. Some people are very adept. Others never get involved. Some would rather give on their own. If there is a hesitancy, usually it comes from fear of doing things incorrectly and ignorance of technique. It is unique, as no other selling job is like it. A knowledge of *education* is essential, at least the use of some of the terminology, and in addition, a detailed acquaintance with the specific school and its program is quite important. Those who have not gone to college feel especially hesitant. However, none of these are impossible hindrances; love of the cause, a working vocabulary which is the result of serious intention in even the popular literature relating to modern education, and a good dose of courage can make any trustee a salesperson.

We at George Fox have learned that everyone responds to in-service training. Some of the content of our board meetings have been given over to actual class sessions, sometimes by using our own talent or by inviting outside experts in a given field. I am convinced that our people, although never previously having these opportunities, have forged ahead of their counterparts from other colleges. I am proud of them. For example, Wilbert Eichenberger distinguishes himself as outstanding among his peers who represent the independent colleges of Oregon. He not only gives weeks of valuable time and energy from the leadership of his firm, he talks of his college in many places, uses his secretary to write good, confirming letters to the right people, has invited many guests to the college, and given stature to the cause. He is a salesman, but he has adapted his techniques to the advantage of George Fox.

Arnold Owen of Berkeley, has done stellar service along the same lines. He has opened door after door for us in the San Francisco area. One of his earliest services was to make a master list for Denver Headrick and me of San Francisco based firms. Early on he hosted a luncheon at his club, and some of the most powerful business magnates of the west coast became acquainted with George Fox. Arnold had done his groundwork well. Through his help, we gained the friendship and respect of people at Crown Zellerbach, Standard Oil of California, California Packing Corporation, Southern Pacific, Bank of California, and others. Both Crown Zellerbach and Southern Pacific continue to be two of our most substantial supporters.

A significant assignment was carried out by teams during one winter when groups went to different churches, showing pictures, giving talks, and answering questions about the college. Mrs. Shambaugh went all over Colorado by herself or sometimes in company with Walter Lee. The Idaho men went from church to church. Phil Martin used his set of pictures both publicly and in his southern California home. Dwight Macy directed an estate of sizable proportions to the college as the principal beneficiary. Dr. Brougher has made a significant contribution in his dealings with drug companies and medical firms, in writing timely letters, and in directing me to the right people at the right time. Clare Willcuts, and Drs. Wayne Roberts and Claude Lewis have provided openings with service clubs, and radio and television audiences. Senator Mark O. Hatfield has spoken in favor of our cause before some very important groups. All of the members, older and new, men and women, have accomplished a splendid service, adding to the prestige of the school. These fine people who serve on the board take pride in their appointment, and their George Fox connection becomes a high avenue of Christian service.

Their involvement in development has been demonstrated over these intervening years, but most consistently in the last twelve. Previous to that, we had no sustained fund raising drive. Under the presidency of Dr. Carey the $25 Club, or Living Endowment was initiated, built up, and sustained. The goal was 1,000 members to generate $25,000 annually. Although it never reached much more than 700, and its best year netted $16,000, still it has proved to be a life saver, for it works much the same as an invested endowment. It has the value of involving a considerable group of stewards in annual support. It has existed for twenty years and it is as strong today as at any time. Due to the ongoing nature of the college drives—ideally, they should never cease—we can chart the steady evolution of one drive followed by another to meet the needs of a growing school. The first of these modern drives was called Advance and its stated purpose was for increased giving to the general fund by anyone in any form. The response from the church constituency and among the alumni was most heartening.

I LEARNED SOME extremely valuable lessons and, if I may be so bold, I think that we all did. My experience was limited in the extreme. True, I had been the pastor of Friends churches, but I was soon to learn that this background could not be construed as being in the same class with college financing. The first lesson was to realize that with confidence and enthusiasm people respond. You do not get the money unless you ask for it. The challenge is to acquaint ourselves with the best methods, to make as few mistakes as possible, so the immediate results will be successful, and the long range benefits will be even greater.

There is a quirk of Quaker personality, a certain reaction, or perhaps it comes from rural pioneering, but we soon learned that to set up a comprehensive program with large challenge totals and defined target dates is not for us. If the college were to mount campaigns to modernize itself, prepare for the future with new buildings and the accompanying material and equipment necessary for higher education today, it would come to millions of dollars. We never did the obvious, adding everything at the bottom of the page. Instead, we charted the immediate future, cut the possibilities into manageable bite-sizes, and made a variety of opportunities available to any person at any one time to give to their unique interest.

Perhaps the biggest lesson of all came in the shocking realization that almost before one drive gets underway another must be envisioned — which led to the Century Club. As may be imagined, the idea was that people would give in units of $100. True, the $25 Club appealed to one set of donors, but should not growing needs of the college demand and expect a larger response of another class with more substantial gifts?

Both the Advance and its successor Century Club provided mainly for the general budget, with some giving designated for specific projects; but it was evident to see that priming pumps for limited objectives would never meet the needs. The malaise of campus facilities engendered a sense of defeat and frustration. In spite of firing the wood furnaces night and day, Wood-Mar was still cold; buckets were used to catch leaks in the library roof while the library staff moved stacks of books to prevent damage and mildew; plumbing was woefully obsolete; walkways were broken up and didn't run where students walked, producing mud everywhere during winter months; dormitories were illheated and lighting was substandard; paint peeled faster than we could put it on. The fall of 1956 found us with no money to do more than maintain ourselves, for with every repair something else would break or wear out or explode. In addition, students had no pleasant place for social life. We were on a treadmill of inefficiency and obsolescence which no amount of crisis maintenance could ever catch us up to the present. We knew that we must somehow break the vicious cycle, replace the worn out with the new, find resources to do things right.

A GREAT DEAL could be said about every improvement and project undertaken to bring our facility up to standard and move forward with new building and development. Creative solutions and group endeavor united us in new ways and generated energy; our experience on one project opened doors for later ones. Early projects set standards and procedures used for future ones as we gained experience and expertise in both building and fund raising.

Recognizing the need for a student gathering place, we worked with First National Bank to put together a package that included $32,000 for a new student union. In part, additional student fees, volunteer or donated labor, and gifts enabled the completion of the fine new building in 1958. This project set up the machinery for the student union board—an experiment in student business management. It also set a precedent for including on the design committee those who will be using the future building.

With these successes firmly in our grasp, we prepared ourselves for the next drive, the Diamond Jubilee—so named because George Fox was celebrating its seventy-fifth year. This drive was for campus improvement including the Shambaugh Library and the Student Union, as well as work on Weesner Village, and Pennington Hall which were primarily financed with a federal loan. The first brochure was prepared by a professional advertising firm using the main theme of "George Fox Is Growing," carrying the diamond symbol throughout. Going over it after all these years, my first reaction is one of "how far we have come!" But the brochure is interesting and instructive in itself. It shows where we were at the time and where we hoped to go. It shows in retrospect, what has been accomplished in the interim, what we have done which was not imagined, and some items yet to be done.

The committee which worked out the features of the library was composed of Dean Kenneth Williams, chair, Genette McNichols, librarian, and division chairs. They worked in close harmony with architect Don Lindgren. His method was to go with me and the committee to view new libraries which had been built on other campuses—University of Portland, Oregon College of Education, Willamette University. Then we fell heir to a tremendous source of information. Brother David at the University of Portland was Genette McNichols' major professor in her master's program and showed a great interest in what was being planned at her college. He had done a comparative study on the architecture and features of some seventeen Catholic college libraries for his doctoral dissertation. He turned all this valuable data over to the committee. What a break!

Gilbert Shambaugh himself turned the first shovelful of dirt in 1961. All kinds of problems were faced by the contractor and by us secondarily. Among other things, the rains came before the basement was completely dug and the big equipment could not negotiate the slippery blue clay. Two crews, working from opposite ends in digging and laying the sewers, misread their transits and after their backfill were forced to take out everything and re-lay the job, for the far end away from the building was higher than the outlet. The vermiculite on the roof was laid in the wet, causing the roof to bulge, and it had to be re-laid after a hearing to determine relative liability. The contractor failed to push the job and it was far from complete when dedication day arrived. However, it was too late to change all of our plans and announcements, so we proceeded, sans shelves, lights, flooring, draperies and all the rest. The building was beautiful and we were proud and excited about the opportunities it opened for our professors and students.

The dean of Oregon State University gave an address in June, 1962. The entire faculty was in academic regalia, for the first time in history other than commencement itself. Each chairperson of a division presented a book from their respective field to symbolically sit on the new shelves. Gilbert Shambaugh himself was an integral part of the ceremony. The a cappella choir rendered its inspired numbers. Of course, hundreds of alumni, supporters, and best-wishers were on hand. Without exactly realizing it, we were establishing elements of our heritage and building up traditions.

One tradition we embraced was the selection of a fitting motto to be displayed in a new building, such as the quote from George Fox, "Let their learning be liberal," placed at the entrance of Shambaugh Library. Another significant practice was to schedule a groundbreaking or dedication at a special event such as Homecoming or May Day. These often involved the people whose contributions (financial or otherwise) were being honored in the building's name. Such events drew members of our constituency as well as college and city leaders, and often featured an address by a distinguished guest such as Governor Mark O. Hatfield, a member of our Board of Trustees.

The use of brick in all our buildings guarantees unity and harmony, while modern methods, materials, and concepts make each one unique. The artistic use of murals, pools, plazas, and plantings incorporated into the construction adds to the effect. An outstanding example is the ceramic mural on the west wall of the Shambaugh Library. It was done in Venetian glass and Byzantine gold mosaic, and is a conception of Christian education. After Shambaugh Library, Pennington Hall, and Weesner Village, building continued with the addition of the next co-ed dorm, Edwards Hall, followed by Heacock Commons dining hall, and Calder Center, offering much-needed classrooms, lecture hall, laboratories, and faculty offices.

So I sum up the consideration of finances and the administration. Our connection with the church will be our next theme.

Chapter five

The Church

WHEN I ANSWERED the call to Christian service at Twin Rocks Conference Center in the summer of 1929, I anticipated that it was the calling for a lifetime, anywhere. I was drawn to the mission field so I continued my training at Bible school, and later my formal education at Willamette University with that aim in view. I was hoping to go to Bolivia where the church was considering a new work and I bent every effort to prepare myself for the coveted goal with a major in Spanish and a minor in international relations. I took one course in anthropology and diplomacy and earned a secondary teaching credential—all to be ready for the right opening if and when it came. My girlfriend, Helen Ritter, had sensed the same call and dedication to it, and we made all of our plans accordingly. Even before our marriage we presented ourselves before the Board of Missions so they would know and consider us for mission service.

Through all the subsequent years, in meetings, in outposts, in both small and large churches, in the city and in the country, even though I have not yet traveled to South America, there has been a growing and widening realization that all service rendered has been, in fact, Christian service and in answer to the divine call. Likewise, in the postal service; in the fruit cannery; in church and parsonage construction; and in later years when I became a union carpenter, following the trade all week and preaching on Sunday.

173

Always it was with a kind of anticipation that I was preparing for something more, something of momentous importance.

If I had followed the preaching advocated in my youth, I dare say that I should have been torn between a restricted view of the ministry as being behind the sacred desk only and the underlying Quaker concept that all service is sacred. Whatever the philosophical bases of my motivation, one would have never imagined I would become a college president. Certainly the struggles of Pacific College during that period of my observation were anything but enticing to a person looking toward a career. The job was simply not attractive to me in any way.

I myself was surprised that my interest in George Fox kept growing. Surely, it could not be for me. Would my call to missionary work be compromised by associating myself with a college, even a church-related college? Was there anything that I could do, any service I could render, because I had not been able to go on to obtain a doctor's degree? I questioned if I could teach and I didn't want to embarrass the board — my impressions were that small colleges had too many ill-prepared misfits already. But all the while I became more interested.

A contributing factor to this growing awareness was our family's connection with the Kings Garden Schools of Seattle. Our two boys both attended and graduated. I heard sermons and lectures there and at Seattle Pacific College which brought to my attention the growing need for dynamic Christ-centered education. Then my son Stephen began to get ready for college and chose George Fox. Helen's illness made it impossible for me to continue in the pastoral ministry and we looked to other avenues of employment and service in deference to her needs. At one point I let Ivan Adams know of my interest in coming to work at the college. Some weeks later, he and Donald McNichols made the trip to Seattle and interviewed me, but nothing came of the offer. We left Seattle and moved to Salem where I built a home. Only after that was I again contacted about joining the staff to assist in student recruitment.

*W*HEN I CAME into the presidency, I had been away from the pastorate for some months working at the carpenter trade to support my family. During this time I was asked to conduct evangelistic services and Bible conferences for various churches. I had already made promises to a number of churches in the Northwest and Colorado to come to them in the winter of 1954-55. I conferred with the board, and they agreed that I should honor the promises and reach as many churches as possible as college president as well as evangelist.

Thus began my ministry in churches as president of George Fox. If I had had one private fear when I came to George Fox, it was that I might not have opportunities to preach, which I coveted. I might have spared myself the fear—I have had many opportunities. I have preached in every church of Oregon Yearly Meeting, and in some of them many times. I have enjoyed a good ministry in Friends churches all over America, in sister denominations, before conventions and union rallies, schools, youth camps, service clubs, and professional meetings.

From the first month, Harlow Ankeny assisted me by preparing slide presentations which I have used in many churches and other public ministry. With hundreds of shots now, we have quite a complete pictorial history: shots of faculty; student life and activities such as special events, ball games, May Day festivities, choir tours, commencement scenes; campus shots before 1957 and before-and-after pictures of new facilities since that time. For new buildings we were able to show first chart and blueprint, followed by construction shots, then conclude with completion, dedication, and actual use. Other series were of outstanding alumni, building up to one of President Herbert Hoover himself taken on campus when we feted him for his eighty-first birthday. Still other series have been created to more effectively tell the story of stewardship between the church and the college: how a college dollar is spent, the charting of a new financial drive, a Christian's estate, membership and enrollment figures, objects for designated giving, and similar themes which can be shown by graphs, charts, or drawings.

One recurring theme of my presentations to various groups has been that Christian education is part of the Great Commission; another, the theology of Christian higher education. For years I have stressed the theme of modern day miracles at George Fox. Another often-used theme has been to present the biblical concept of adult responsibility to the next generation. The Scripture used was Psalms 145:4 which reads, "One generation shall praise thy works to another, and shall declare thy mighty acts." The idea here is that entrenched ways of thinking can be changed by starting with children and youth.

Each professor has had a unique ministry, never dictated by me, but acceptable in different kinds of audiences. Paul Mills has emphasized Bible studies and evangelism, and since his travels around the world, missions and archeology. Myron Goldsmith is greatly given to inspirational messages from the New Testament. Everett Craven preaches on Christian education. Dr. Roberts is so resourceful and novel as to deny simple categorization. One of his most interesting, however, is the development of the theme of ways the church differs from its college. Earl Craven was forceful in the pulpit, and likewise, Dr. Kennison, Jerry Louthan, and Frank Furtado as athletes. Sheldon Louthan is outstanding as a vocalist, even presenting full concerts to large and enthusiastic audiences. And I cannot omit the blessing which the testimony of our campus workers has brought: Alice Dixon, Elsie Hermanson Campbell, Stuart Richey, Isaac Smith, Joseph Reece, and Ward Haines.

While all of this illustrates the impact of the simple, informal relation to the church, a repeated theme has developed which, although not planned, has permeated much of what has been done and said. It is that the college is the feeder and fountainhead of other good works. Ministers receive their biblical studies, while missionaries learn foreign languages, sociology, anthropology, and international relations. Doctors, lawyers, and professional leaders take their under-graduate studies and teachers pass through its doors and go out to train the minds of young people, not only in public schools but as leaders in church schools, Sunday schools, youth camps, and related activities. The list can go on into every walk of life—missions, agriculture, population, health, peace and war, education, rights, and law.

In its relationship to the church, the college thus becomes vitally important. It is a kind of head to the body. While the analogy breaks down in that the body without the head is dead, the church without the college surely will be hindered: it can become eccentric or go off on tangents because of ill-prepared leadership, it tends to lose its unique character, it ceases to renew itself.

I THINK OF George Fox College as the last true hope of the Society of Friends." I lift the quotation out of a letter to me from Dr. Howard Kershner, president of the Christian Freedom Foundation of New York City. I hesitated to use it primarily because it may be considered too extravagant. All the same, it represents the kind of appraisal which is coming from people of his calibre, who because of their wide experience and understanding of Christian movements, might look only too lightly on a little college hidden in a small town in western Oregon, but who instead come to a conclusion which prompts a statement such as this.

Often there is a kind of subjective devotion which places a halo over everything in which a person is engaged. It is all too easy to come up with the notion that what a person is interested in merits the same concern and attention from everyone else. It is a temptation—often fallen into among religious enthusiasts—to build little empires around their enterprises, thus creating organizations out of proportion to the intrinsic value or relative importance to the kingdom of God. Individuals can become so engrossed in activity toward desired ends that all other projects lose their appeal, not only to themselves, but in an extension of their views over to what they think others should cherish. The result is a ladder of priorities with the topmost place being usurped by one's own interest, and all others, however important to Christianity or to humanity, are of necessity relegated to inferior positions on the lower rungs.

I eschew any such attitude. I do not espouse it for myself or for my interests. I trust that God will continue to give me enough tolerance and breadth of understanding to know that his kingdom is greater than any of its parts, that there is a place for all consecrated service, and that there is a happy combination of talent and need. People should love their work and throw themselves into it. All during my Christian life I have been motivated by a desire to do the will of God.

The relationship between the church and college is a two-way street. There is a cliché which was first used to describe the position of eager denominations in relation to their fledgling colleges in the nineteenth century, and it is still apropos, "Strong on founding them but weak in supporting them."

As a pastor in my early ministry, I admit to being abysmally ignorant of the costs of operating a college. To average church members, it may appear cheaper to get return on a dollar in some other way. Attractive advertising shows how a few cents a day can feed a waif. Evenings and Saturdays are spent assisting with a church building project which costs only a few thousand dollars. Giving for a mission project can be encompassed with a day's wage. By comparison, a college fund drive with a goal of millions of dollars leaves them numb.

It may be that the earnest church member should look within to discern motives for how and to whom money is given. There are many faithful believers in enlightened America who have little or no concept of the tremendous strategic value of the church college to the church. Lacking this understanding and therefore devoid of a commitment, they are not challenged to extend themselves to support one of the greatest partners the church has ever had. They do not see the Christian enterprise in its entirety.

*T*HERE HAVE BEEN many stories on American campuses of compromise—of selling out—pointing to a wealthy patron as the culprit. I think, after these years, that I understand some of the pressures and how they present a subtle temptation. It can be shown that highly opinionated and even cantankerous millionaires have been overly influential. I testify to the glory of God that he has given me courage to withstand to this present day. Just such situations, however, have bred distrust, broken down confidence, cut off the chain of prayer support, and dried up the springs of stewardship.

It is possible, when one is approached in ways which might lead to spiritual compromise, to stand one's ground, defend one's self, win friends, and perhaps still obtain the money. I like millionaires! I like them as persons as well as for what they can accomplish with their resources. I know that God can do more with a dollar than a penny. It may give us pause to realize that some Christians may hold to different sets of rules and social standards but we need not turn prospective donors away if they disagree. Those who handle wealth are no different from anyone else, except that they may be very shrewd and clever; they are open to reasonable discussion; they have ability to ascertain.

All of what I am saying was made clear to me most vividly when I look back to a significant conversation in my office several years ago. It was during a period when a number of community leaders were considering the possibility of establishing a junior college in Newberg and some debated the appeal of George Fox to the average high school graduate. Was it popular to attend George Fox? Did we offer enough majors? Was our ban on social dancing and drinking a hindrance to the growth of the college? I was discussing these questions with a leading citizen who had access to funds for educational purposes. Very evidently he did not agree with the fairly rigid stand at George Fox. Very honestly too, his church made no such demands upon him and his family. Would it not be better for all concerned for the administration at the college to loosen up a bit, thus becoming more attractive to the average American youth, parents, and general public? There followed a long and detailed argument on my part as to why I felt it was best to hold the line. At the end he said, quite emphatically, "Well, if you keep those archaic views, the college will never grow and you will never get any of my money!" We parted cordially enough, but I knew we were miles apart in our opinions.

The next several days were very difficult indeed! The college was desperately in need of funds. We had to enroll more students. We must secure more community support. After all, no one need ever know what I had told my interviewer. Perhaps the church, my church, was too strict. He was an active communicant of another church. But through it all there came to me a sense of peace and repose. As we saw it, there was truth and meaning to our standards. I had no right to change them. If I could not agree, it was for me to resign rather than to sell out. I tried to dismiss the entire episode from my mind, but that was easier said than done. The immediate problem was solved, however, when in less than a month he presented the college with a check for $25,000!

But the problem is not solved forever by one check! True, this one episode had concluded satisfactorily for all parties. I had remained faithful to my beliefs, the standards and practices of the college were not compromised; I had made a genuine friend, and our material needs were being met. One way of looking at the general problem, one step down from the high theological and philosophical plane, is to stoically admit that in administration, whatever one does, one makes both friends and enemies. What wins one repels another. What gains support robs from another cause. One cannot gain the loyalty, support, affection, and respect of every person. It follows that whatever I might have done, irrespective of my integrity or any other principles involved, would not be satisfactory to all. What if I had made promises which, if carried out, would have lost me the confidence of the church? What if I had taken in one $25,000 only to lose another? What if I had so changed the social patterns as to appeal to ten more students only to lose ten others with different ideals for their college?

*M*Y FIRST TOUCHSTONE was to order the affairs of the college to ensure divine favor. I am aware that Christian obedience does not guarantee a cessation of trouble and difficulty. There is a spurious teaching today among sincere Christians that God will reward with success any who are true to conscience and invite God into their enterprise. Scripture suggests that the godly will suffer persecution. The problem may be in our obedience and commitment as much as in our misunderstanding of the ways of God. I am brought back to the question of divine favor, not so much as a formula for success but as a way of daily living, whatever the outcome may be. Therefore we will order the affairs of the college seeking to know the will of God generally and specifically, and pray for power and grace to be obedient to that will.

One does not have to look far to find prosperous institutions whose commitment is anything but Christian, where the climate does not appear to be conducive to holy living, and the bias of professors is negative and destructive to students' faith. At the same time, we find colleges that are committed to honor Christ and integrate their disciplines into the concept of divine truth who struggle with lack of funding, inadequate facilities, and low visibility. The contrast is not fiction.

In this light, I elect to put plans and decisions to the test. The major plans and programs must answer to the question, "Is it to God's glory?" All lesser issues must also prove themselves with the query, "What would Jesus do?" Every difficult decision finds its justification in a divine mandate. We make the best decision possible to bring excellence to George Fox and honor to God.

*T*HE IDEAL Christian college enhances and deepens the spiritual life of its youth. It is probably the best known religious environment available to the church today. Especially is it the case in a campus-type, residential school where students are surrounded by an intentional well-ordered environment. This environment so powerfully reinforces spiritual values, nothing else in the program of the church or our current society can anywhere approximate it. Nothing else can equal the totality of hours, much less what those hours contain. Then, taking these precious hours, add to them their rich content: godly professors, a great concentration of Christian youth, a combination of religious and intellectual stimulus, a minimum of negative factors, the witness of everyone from the president to the cooks and gardeners, the coordination of ideal elements leading to integrated living such as athletics and parties and other social events; all add to a tremendous impact on youth right at the time when it is most needed.

The years from seventeen to twenty-two are climactic in the maturation of young people. Social pressures are strong. It is the age of doubt. The direction of one's life calling is often found and perhaps prepared for. Sex becomes a powerful quest. Life-long habits and friendships solidify. But I think the greatest force is found in molding and filling out one's philosophy of life: who am I, what will I do, where am I going? Right when one is questioning and doubting everything, rejecting parents and launching out, when so much of the past is up for suspicion and the future to fear, it is ideal to find oneself with models of faith.

Dr. Bernard Ramm, of Covina Baptist Seminary, said in chapel that he doubted a glib interpretation of the teaching of King Solomon: "Train up a child in the way that he should go, and when he is old, he will not depart from it." He said the old proverb may work well enough until one goes off to college, and then one strong set of pressures exerted by a heretic professor, and all can be lost!

It is difficult to analyze the strongest factors in building a satisfactory adult faith. Surely the structure of the case is important: godly teachers, integrated education, the policies of the trustees, a kind of reputation and image. All are essential. It is ideal to have religious emphases once or twice a year, and we know at George Fox that many youth, some even from a non-Christian background, have accepted Christ as Savior and Lord during these times. We appreciate the times when church vocations are presented. Daily chapels, when rightly conducted, are a constant challenge to measure up to the divine law. Prayer meetings deepen the spiritual life of students. Deputation teams give expression and a ready outlet for trained enthusiasm. All types of events may contribute to the development of faith and character.

It has been found that the values gained from one's experiences at a Christian college may not be those from formal or planned confrontations, but rather from quiet talks with a roommate or friend, a devotional time early in the morning, or a chance remark by a professor. The total environment of an ideal Christian college is to be sought after and exploited to the full. This is the church's great ally.

The intellectual life is equally as important. Eager freshmen are mistaken indeed if they imagine a Christian college to be nothing more or less than an elongated Youth for Christ rally. The business of a college, any college, and most emphatically a Christian college is to educate. If there was an unwanted legacy inherited from the past, it was that spiritual environment may be coveted more than getting an education. Of course, this was not universally true nor had the professors so designed it. The truth is, however, that not many intellectual giants had stayed to graduate at Pacific or George Fox in the last generation. We worked hard to produce a climate for intellectual growth. For the church needs that kind of member in its pews, that kind of leadership at its helm, and that kind of witness in today's world.

THERE ARE A number of areas in which the college influences or leads the church; however, the most obvious benefit comes through theology. When one reviews church history, one finds many prototypes of what the church-related college should mean today, from ancient schools of the prophets through rabbinical schools at the time of our Lord's earthly ministry. This continued in the Judaic tradition through the Diaspora and Talmudic periods, and over into the Christian church to Alexandria and Carthage and the monastic schools of the Dark Ages, on up to the university centers of Europe—and especially for our consideration—which became Lutheran or Reformed or Anglican or Free.

The American liberal arts college was founded to produce clergy. Denominational colleges and seminaries become part of a strong foundation of the church, training the next generation of church leaders all over the world. In the modern educational sense, grouping of theological experts and spiritual leaders onto a college campus is the most reasonable and efficient use of their minds which can be imagined. These talents energize one another. The church is enriched. Rather than being taken away from pastorates or other assignments, thus leaving a vacuum in manpower needs of the church, they are being strategically placed to the best use conceivable.

I have often said that George Fox has the strongest religion faculty of any Quaker college. The church has shown divine wisdom in releasing these keen biblical scholars and placing them in an environment with the opportunity to affect the future of the faith. A study made in 1965 showed that one-fifth of all Quaker youth preparing for church callings anywhere in the United States were to be found enrolled at George Fox. This is in itself quite an enviable record, to say nothing of an awesome obligation. Where better could these professors exercise their callings?

Each generation faces fresh challenges aimed at the institutional church and its orthodoxy. This age is no different. Attacks on the church and against the faith are world-wide, terrifically virulent, and highly successful. Foes are without and within, and strangely enough, some of the greatest foes of the second half of the twentieth century are those who should be its friends and staunchest advocates—bishops and preachers and theologians and other alleged Christians. Its foes are not so much, as in other periods of conflict, found among the outsiders, the atheists, and the scientists. Strange as it may seem today, these "outsiders" are as often as not the ones who are coming forward saying some very worthwhile things about faith and practice.

The world-wide battle is aimed primarily at the minds of youth. The Christian college has something to say in the struggle. In the words of Dr. Daniel C. Poling, "The greatest mission field in the world today is found in the minds of our keenest youth." True, not all of these keen youth will be found on church college campuses, but we conceive of those who are as belonging to cell groups, highly important to affect society for good. These are the ones we are preparing to be theologically literate.

TO REINFORCE the idea that the college leads or helps the church, I refer to the important 1966 Danforth Study, "Church Sponsored Higher Education in the United States," under Dr. Manning Pattillo, in which the authors say:

> It is time for colleges to turn their attention to the churches that have nurtured them and not merely regard the churches as sources of students and money. The grave problems faced by the churches have already been outlined. To reverse or redirect or adapt to a change in world view as profound as that through which we are passing cannot be simple. It may take a century for the church to chart its course of action.

> We cannot expect church administrators and pastors to give the answers. They are too much involved in the day-to-day activities of the church. They are called upon to work out ad hoc solutions to immediate problems. They are supposed to inspire others; they must not admit to discouragement or perplexity. This role precludes the dispassionate examination of large historical and philosophical trends in perspective — the work necessary to frame proposals commensurate with the church's problems. Nor does it seem likely that the needed guidance can come from seminary faculties and professional theologians. The manpower available in theological schools is too meager and its outlook necessarily limited.

> In our judgment the faculties of church-related colleges are in the most favorable position to provide intellectual leadership in the study of issues facing the church and to hammer out proposals for action. The church college lives in both the "church world" and the "outside world." Its faculty, in the

aggregate, has the breadth of knowledge required to see the
church in perspective. College faculties include historians,
philosophers, artists, theologians, psychologists, sociolo-
gists, literary critics, political scientists, and economists—
scholars whose business it is to be sensitive to ideas and to
understand the meaning of the world around us. They are in
touch with secular thought, but at their best they care about
the church and its future.

We urge faculties of church-affiliated institutions to view
themselves as scholarly task forces for assessing the status
of the Christian church in the changed and changing world.
Let the faculties do in a more comprehensive and thorough
way the kind of diagnosis we have attempted in this report.
It is not now being done on a systematic basis. Let them
make their scholarly contribution to the sound development
of Christian social thought—a requisite in this age of turbu-
lence. Some colleges are already providing certain types of
leadership to the churches, but much more is required.

I say, "Amen!"

The church as well as its college must have a strategy. It must
have a set of priorities. What can we learn from history along these
lines? One truth which comes out of the pages of the past is that
the church has prospered most during periods of appreciation of
learning. The Judeo-Christian ethic provides for the education of
youth. We have the law of Moses, and we have illustrations out of
the New Testament with characters such as Paul, Luke, and others.

The Christian church took on the task, not only of educat-
ing each succeeding generation, but of becoming a repository of
wisdom and learning. The monastic movement kept the light of
learning burning during the Dark Ages. Most churches had schools
attached to them. These schools later became the cells from which
the great universities grew. There is a close correlation between the
flowering of the church and the flowering of learning.

SIMILARLY, WE CAN SEE this in even a cursory study of the missionary movement and its earlier dependence upon Christian colleges and universities for its candidates. The roster of names includes James Richards, Francis Robbins, Harvey Loomis, Gordon Hall, Luther Rice, Byram Green, and Samuel Nott at the Williams College Haystack prayer meeting; David J. Livingston at Edinburgh; Stubbs at Yale; Billy Graham at Wheaton. This body of evidence demonstrates that the extension of the church, both at home and abroad, frequently stems directly from the institution, teaching, and environment of the Christian college.

Until I was at least forty years of age, these concepts were new to me and I had never thought them through, nor had they become a part of my personal philosophy. I had heard quips such as "If you can't preach, teach," which did nothing to improve my opinion of Christian education. I had heard Dean Gregory, our general superintendent, give a message on the floor of Oregon Yearly Meeting in which he claimed it was the duty of the church and not the state to educate its youth. I did not accept his thesis and at that point thought him radical.

More and more, however, by my directed reading, by attention to skilled advocates of the idea, by my working together with other Christian educators, by the evident poverty of public education which excluded God, and, no doubt, by the direct leadership of the Holy Spirit, I have come to be highly convinced and deeply committed to the position that Christian education is the task of the church. I use the term to include formal, week day schooling at all levels, including college and not simply Sunday school and youth meetings.

IN 1962 I SHARED with Oregon Yearly Meeting ministers my concerns regarding the role of the Christian college in the life of the church. Perhaps it serves as a summary of my commitment to students, to the college, and to my church.

A school such as George Fox meets our youth at a very tumultuous age—in adolescence when doubts are beginning to come to the fore, at their first experiences away from home, with heavy social and sex drives, and at the time when you have had your "fill" of them at home, or would be experiencing troubles if they were to stay home. All these attitudes and situations are aggravated by homesickness, social clashes, finances, and the fact that college is more difficult than high school. Some are in revolt. Some are seeing the expression of latent talents. Even the best of born-again Christian youth may have lived a very sheltered life previous to going away to college, having made few decisions, and being quite innocent of the world at large.

The average pastor and church endeavor to appeal to youth. This is done by all kinds of happy experiences, bending over backwards to entice attendance, to produce a pleasurable experience, to build around them interest and enjoyment. Young people are greeted with the impression that they are doing the church a big favor in attendance. They are complimented on showing up. Sunday school is generally not a very serious pursuit. We are guilty of even presenting the claims of the gospel as producing joy, thrill, happiness, and success. Ministers very seldom cross a youth except in minor social infractions such as whispering in the back seat of the church. The pastor, or youth director, is happy to welcome them ten minutes late to any meeting and dismiss them after a session. The church makes no claim to responsibility after the meeting is dismissed. The problems of social adjustment, obedience, work in school, responsibility, finances, what they do with their time, are all secondary. The average exposure to church in formal meetings is never more than five or six hours a week and many times is much less, even to an hour at Sunday school. All are welcome. No questions are asked. The boy who smokes or drinks is most welcome, or should be. I believe in these evangelistic and social concerns.

But the college faces altogether different social and intellectual pressures. We take on a student twenty-four hours a day, seven days a week. Our problems begin when the church lets go. We tell them that life is serious. There may be little satisfaction at the moment in studying half the night for an examination. They are not complimented in showing up for an examination at the beginning of a class period. All kinds of mental, spiritual, and physical disciplines are imposed, and many of these must be motivated from within the person of the student. They must get up for breakfast— there is no mother who brings it to the bedroom, or who lets them indulgently live off French fries and cokes. There is no one to tell them to study. If they make the team, or a play, or the choir, or the honors program, it is up to them. We cannot countenance social excesses.

But we are not harsh in these situations. We counsel with all students academically and spiritually. Our deans give countless hours to all who have need. They are on hand day and night. The faculty meets weekly to pray over the youth. A spirit of concern pervades the entire campus and opportunities are given for spiritual growth at every turn. It is popular to do right.

The college takes the position that our administration of disciplines must be in the vanguard of the church's stand. We owe such a position to Christ and his church. We cannot allow ourselves to dissipate into a more common institution, degenerating with the Laodicean age, and lowering the standards with every student generation. Youth are the leaders of tomorrow and their spiritual disciplines, their social patterns, their viewpoints on life, their integrity should become habitual during their college years. We trust that our endeavors, although borne in spiritual travail for them, will eventuate in a more spiritual church, in leadership in our world which will protect it from its mad tobogganing toward Armageddon, and in homes of love and stability.

We cannot let every girl dress like she has at home. We cannot allow every boy to squirrel around like he did before coming to college. We must insist that if a passing grade is to be given, the student must show up to class and write papers on time. It is quite a shock to many students to accept the fact that a professor is still a true Christian after having given an "F" in a course. We cannot smile upon staying out at all hours, even though they did at home. We cannot give permission to unchaperoned parties even when parents did not crack down previously. Nor do we set up programs which allow trips to far distant places over weekends. We do not allow medical excuses for sleeping in on Monday morning.

A local church needs to work along with the majority, either fast or slow. Even church architecture shows the desire to give in to the more affluent members. But a college sets the tone for tomorrow. The faculty's competence and training, professional leadership, Christian faith, and consistency all go along with the facilities in which they operate, the genuineness and integrity of the institution. When decisions are made with reasonableness, when students actually learn, when progress is made, when success is evident, when excellence is achieved — all these factors determine the direction of a student's life. The opposite is true. If requirements are slovenly, if toilets are leaking, if buildings are not heated, if the faculty is not paid, if a book needed for the library cannot be afforded, if the church does not in fact support the college, if a good professor leaves — all these factors cast a pall over the operation and affect the student negatively, perhaps for all of life, and eternity.

The conditions which we long for in the church twenty years from now are in embryo form at the college today. It is for such reasons that we are deeply concerned about the excellence of our service now.

OUR HISTORY reaches back to the Quakers of Newberg who established the school and were diligent in overseeing it. The relationship of the college to the church was deeply embedded. From the early years the college has supported the Friends Church in a number of ways, some long-term, others short-term; some well-planned and some very casual; some in cooperation with church leaders while some were carried out by our own staff or students.

Professors from the George Fox religion department initiated the Pastors Short Course in serious biblical studies. Schools for the Elders followed as another avenue of help to local church leaders, working through quarterly meetings. The college also worked to help the yearly meeting programs that involved youth, by sending music and leadership teams to camps, vacation Bible schools, and other church programs, and encouraging college youth to participate in the summer Youth Ambassador program serving a specific local church. Individual professors also have had many opportunities for personal ministry, often being invited to preach, teach, or share musical talents while others shared their testimony in other ways. Prayer bulletins have encouraged the churches to support specific needs of the college.

A Christian church-related college might be ideally described in this way: The college is committed to honor Christ and to instill in its graduates a love for the church and a willingness to give themselves to sacrificial callings. Its professors are knowledgeable in their fields and endeavor to integrate their disciplines into the total concept of divine truth. They take as a divine charge that God has placed in their hands the grand scheme of Christian enlightenment. The future of the church is given over to them. There is a holy trust. The major plans and programs are called upon to justify their existence wholly with an affirmative answer to the question: "Is it to God's glory?"

Appendix A

Family History

compiled by Dennis Hagen

T HE OREGON TRAIL has been revered by many families who trace their roots to enterprising couples who decided to leave the East and Midwest to come to Oregon Country. Though the first migration of size came West as early as 1843, the trail was used until the end of the century. So it was natural for the Scottish Ross family to come West on the trail from Custer County, Nebraska, to Brownsville, Oregon, in the year 1890. Milo's father Clifton was a lad of nine years when the family set out with two wagons, a top buggy, and thirteen head of horses. The trip took three and one-half months.

When Clifton was twenty-seven, he married Carrie Prince. Her family also came to Oregon in 1890 from Maine where she was born. Her mode of travel was by train when she was only three weeks old. Carrie was eighteen years old when she married Clifton and she brought a rich family heritage that went back to the Mayflower landing in 1620.

The Society of Mayflower Descendants in the state of Oregon publishes a small handbook that lists descendants, the name of the individual ancestor on board the ship, and the number of generations between the two. In the 1975-77 publication, there are 154 names listed as descendants who are members of the society. Of these, only six are direct descendants of four or more of the Mayflower shipmates and Carrie Prince Ross is one of them.

193

So it was that Milo Ross with Scottish heritage from his father's side and English ancestry traced back to the Mayflower on his mother's side, was born in 1911 in Salem, Oregon. It would be his privilege to someday lead one of America's ten Quaker colleges where he would work with others for the ordering, preservation, and furtherance of a Quaker school. Like the Mayflower Compact, he too would enact, constitute, and frame various ordinances and acts that would provide a framework of order and stability for a modern college to survive "for the glory of God and advancement of the Christian faith."

Milo had an older sister named Doryce who was a keen observer of his early years. When asked to provide anecdotes of their childhood, she was able to write extensively about not only his life, but also about their parents. There is much humor in these stories and they give insight into characteristics of Milo's personality. For those who knew Milo well as a pastor or college president, they will see a number of connections between his adult traits and those described here when he was a child.

One of these traits was working with his hands—first as a carpenter, and secondly as a gardener. In these anecdotes, aspects of Milo's stern father and compassionate but hard working mother are also clearly described. These stories by Doryce Ross Fraser provide a window to the reader into what it was like growing up in the years of 1915 to 1930. Milo was known as Mike at home, and Doryce uses that name often. She concludes her writing with a few comments about his marriage to Helen Ritter and her difficult health problems.

The Family Story

told by Doryce Ross Fraser

OUR PARENTS, grandparents, teachers, and probably the ministers, called my brother Milo. Everyone else called him Mike. General use of the name Milo was unknown to me until I visited him in Newberg. Perhaps his friends and associates used it after he became an adult and minister. I was not living in the area and had not heard it. Our father did not like nicknames and he selected the name Milo saying, "No one can nickname that." Mom said that one of the first visitors to the home after Mike's birth said, "And how is little Mikie today?"

We had a built-in wood box on the back porch and Mike was expected to keep it full. Dad cut the wood and Mike brought it in. Our first cousin, Harriette Winslow, visited us recurrently from Tillamook. She was about five years younger than Mike and doted on him. Mike would crawl into the wood box with Harriette and read to her, tell her stories, and just be together quietly.

The folks did the gardening in the beginning. Mike showed a real interest and love of gardening, so he took over Dad's part at an early age. He was very proud of his vegetables and fruits. This love for growing things continued throughout his life. He was always finding a sprig of something new and he subsequently wanted everyone to share his joy at the flower it produced. The yard was filled with many choice blooms.

MILO WENT to Grant Junior High from the fall of 1922 to the spring of 1925. He rarely missed a day in school and was not tardy according to attendance records. His best subjects were history, art, and manual training. He was also a good speller. He earned average grades in English, mathematics, writing, and music. His most difficult class was physical education.

Fred Remington, one of Milo's classmates in junior high, shared the following incident.

> Mike and I were both about twelve, and together were leaving the school. It was a rainy day. From out of nowhere the school bully approached Mike and said, "Come on! Get those fists up and fight me!"
>
> Quickly, Milo said, "No, I don't want to fight you or anybody else!"
>
> The bully insisted, "Come on! Are you a sissy?!" What's the matter?"
>
> Milo said, "No, I'm no sissy, but I am a Christian and I simply don't want to fight. I want us to be at peace with each other."
>
> This infuriated the bully and he plunged at Milo, socking him viciously in the face! Yes, he knocked Milo to the ground. Milo came up gasping for breath, with his nose and mouth bleeding profusely.
>
> During the fracas, the bully had dropped his books into the mud. Immediately Milo reached down and picked up the bully's books and said, "I'm sorry you dropped these. I sure hope they aren't ruined."
>
> Milo then turned to pick up his own from the mud. The bully turned, without a word, and stalked away. What a lesson in self control, courtesy, and yes, the grace of God—all given by Milo Ross that day!

Mike loved to make things with wood and was given a coping saw when he was quite young. By the time he was in junior high school, he was making some attractive gifts. I still have the cedar chest he made me in his ninth grade manual training class. This ability and interest stayed with him through life as he became a journeyman carpenter while living in Medford. He could make good, attractive, useful cabinetry and was quite imaginative in details. He never started with sub-standard materials.

*T*HE FOLKS BELONGED to Highland Friends Church and we were taken to all the services from infancy. Dad was the clerk of the meeting and Mom often served as chair of the social committee. We frequently kept an evangelist for two weeks at our home. The folks didn't own a car until 1928 so we always walked. Actually, it was less than a mile to the church so this was not a problem. In fact, Dad would not drive to church even after he bought our first car. Waste of gas! At various times Dad was Sunday school superintendent and he always paid us for memorizing the Ten Commandments, books of the Bible, and portions of Scripture. Those had to be said aloud in front of the assembled group. The Ten Commandments netted us fifty cents. I don't remember receiving money from Dad for any other reason.

Dad was a great storyteller, and I suppose Mike inherited some of that ability from him. There were no televisions (Dad would not allow one in the house) and our family only bought a radio when Mike was about fifteen or sixteen. Dad read us stories from the *Youth's Companion*. We loved those family times. I don't remember ever seeing Dad watch television, although he may have relented in his later years. He read without glasses until his ninety-ninth year — mostly Zane Grey and cowboy stories.

When Mike was in high school, it was the style to get a pair of cream-colored cords in the fall and wear them to school the entire year without washing. The cords became so dirty that they would stand alone. Mom could not stand this and washed Mike's during Christmas vacation. He was outraged — said he would be the laughing stock of the entire school — but he survived.

SINCE WE grew up in a fruit-producing area, we started picking berries at an early age. I can remember walking to Richie's farm—about a mile. When Mike was ten and picking strawberries, he was very serious about this task and worked diligently. We could get home early in the afternoon after a six to eight hour day—hot, dirty, and tired. When we began picking loganberries, Mom joined us and often we picked prunes in the fall. I don't think we tried high fruits like cherries or peaches. When Mike was old enough (we could work eight hours in the canneries at age fourteen), he went to work in the warehouse at Hunts Cannery. He hated this job and the next spring, without the family's knowledge, he applied for a job at Butler's Sign Painting Shop. This must have been the spring before his senior year. He never returned to the cannery as far as I know.

Mike was always honest, but never very clever about handling money. People trusted him, however, and I believe at one time he was the treasurer of four different organizations. He never banked any of these funds, but always kept them in separate piles on the plate rack at home. Periodically I threatened to "straighten out the mess" if he did not move the money elsewhere. One day he discovered all the money was gone. Mike really lost control of himself and began complaining, "Everybody is against me, nobody loves me!" and on and on. After he reached a high pitch and it seemed as though he would suddenly explode, the money mysteriously reappeared. Not long before his death I asked him how he had ever conquered his money phobias. He said, "Oh, I never have. I always have an accountant or consultant check all money matters daily."

IT IS HARD to believe at this point in time that Mike was ever shy. He was extremely so—almost withdrawn—and would hide out when unexpected visitors came to the house. Mom had a paternal uncle who was never able to hold a job because he was so fearful of people, and she feared Mike was going to follow Uncle Fred's pattern. I don't remember Mike ever going on a date with a girl until his senior year of high school, and even then it would have been the latter part of the year as he used to walk me to and from high school performances and there was no girl involved. On the other hand, I think he had some interest in the girls in the church young people's group — particularly a couple of them.

A whole new era of Mike's life developed in his senior year of high school. His history teacher Ralph Bailey recommended that Mike become a member of the school debate team. He said he knew Mike would not compete, but that he had an analytical mind and would be a good debater. The principal was hesitant, but finally agreed. As a debater, he joined classmate Annabel Tooze to debate Corvallis on the question, "Resolved, that Oregon should adopt an integrated system of executive and administrative reorganization along lines of plans recently adopted in a number of American states." Their team took the affirmative position and beat their opponents 3–0. They debated with the team against Dallas and won a unanimous decision of victory by the judges in that contest. Since Mike was an excellent debater, he was chosen to be one of the speakers on the commencement program.

Mike also helped organize the Techne Art Club and became its first president. This club was organized for the purpose of promoting interest in fine arts and of developing fraternity among art students. Membership was limited to thirty-five students with qualifications being satisfactory grades, high quality of original projects, sociability, and a passing grade in the tryout exams. Programs included guest lectures by local artists, expositions, club projects, picnics, and poster campaigns.

He played in one of the productions of the Snikpoh Dramatic Society and was art editor of the *Snikpoh Clarion*, the high school annual. All of this occurred in his senior year and consequently he became the focus of attention of many young women. The most ardent relationship occurred with a young woman named Thelma. Because of her high-strung qualities, a Chevy coupe was later named Thelma. How unpredictable she was!

When Mike entered Salem High School, he continued as an average student in math while retaining his love of art. Biology was hard for him that year but he received an above average grade in French. As a junior, the French slipped one grade, but English had risen to the top along with his favorites of art and history. He received an average grade in typing. His senior year continued with good grades in English and history and an unusual number of activities. He acted in the play, "We've Got to Have Money" in the role of Professor Brigley of Columbia University.

He also participated as assistant *Clarion* (yearbook) manager and art editor, in the Song and Yell contest, in the superior English class, and as speaker for the senior class at commencement. His address was entitled, "Another Milestone," and was given on June 1, 1928. For some reason he lists his hobby as Mexican Athletics in the yearbook of his senior year. Perhaps he had a twinkle in his eye when he made the entry.

Genevieve Beckett Smith went to high school with Milo and she shares her memories of Milo's Christian faith and his humor.

> Milo was a Christian teenager and never ashamed to let his friends know. At church he was the natural leader in our Christian Endeavor group. We had monthly socials which included caroling at Christmas, going on outings to parks, and Sunday afternoon walks often accompanied by Milo playing on a ukulele while we sang. He was wholesome, happy, and fun to be with.
>
> Saturday night parties in the church basement included well-planned games followed by refreshments. Often we used Scriptures or Bible characters in our games. One memorable night someone had Proverbs 9:4 — new to all of us. Now, just outside the front door of Highland Friends Church was a large blackboard used to announce special items of interest or speakers for the day, but often there was nothing on it. After the basement was cleaned up and we were leaving, Milo took a piece of chalk and wrote in his bold print our new Scripture, "Whoso is simple, let him turn in hither." We all laughed and went our separate ways.

The next morning when we gathered for Sunday school the board was clean. Nothing was said. But in the morning sermon our good pastor waxed quite eloquent on the signs of the times when men would blaspheme the very sanctuary of the church with ridicule and he told what he had found when he arrived early that morning. He went on to say that he knew it was not a young person because young people in that day could not write that well! Needless to say, at the close of the service we gathered around pastor Edgar P. Sims and confessed, trying to assure him we were all in on it and only meant it as a prank with no thought of ridicule.

MIKE AND I both thought Dad was a very difficult person with whom to live. He worked diligently and always provided for us, but he didn't believe in any frills. If I received a compliment he would say, "Don't let it go to your head, girl." On the other hand, he was quite a favorite outside the home. On his mail route he was given many Christmas gifts—all of which were locked up in his rolltop desk. Candy was carefully doled out after Christmas. He did not enjoy Christmas, but I suppose he was exhausted from the extra work. I still meet people who talk about the candy corn Dad gave them at Sunday school or church, although Mike and I were not allowed this treat. It was always an embarrassment to us that Dad never carried any money in his pocket. If some family took us on a picnic and there was a charge for the picnic grounds, he did not pay the fee. His attitude was if you have anything with you, it will be spent.

Dad's belief was that the man of the house was automatically the head while Mom's was that this was a position to be earned. She was quick-witted and often outmaneuvered Dad. They never agreed on much of anything.

Dad himself had not had the opportunity for schooling beyond the third grade. However, he went to high school before and after marriage and improved his knowledge. There was never any question in our house regarding going to college. This was taken for granted.

Dad always ridiculed Mom's heritage. She was a smart woman and had a full Latin scholarship to Willamette University when she graduated from Salem High School in 1908. However, she wanted to change her lifestyle so she quit college to get married. Dad always encouraged Mom to return to college — particularly when Mike and I were at Willamette — but Mom never had the courage to go back. Her father, Charles Lester Prince, had been a brilliant linguist at Bates College in Maine back in the 1880s.

I don't really know much about my paternal relations. My grandfather and grandmother Ross were divorced when Dad was about seventeen years old. They had come to the Brownsville area via the Oregon Trail in 1890. Dad came to Salem with his mother in about 1902 and cut himself off from his father. His mother was a fastidious woman and an excellent cook. She loved beautiful things and was a Friends minister. She had a very strange personality and disposition. When she remarried, Dad thought this was against Scripture and felt personally disgraced. He did care for her in her final illness in Salem. His father made contact with us when Mike was about twelve, and we met our Dad's half-sister, Glenda. Grandpa Ross had remarried a very fine woman whom we called "Aunt Mary." We visited them in Brownsville two or three times. He died in 1932.

Dad's rolltop desk was a source of much tension in the home. It took up too much space in the living room and other furniture had to be placed around it. All of us except Dad hated it. When he moved into Friendsview Manor and I was asked if I wanted it, I said, "No way! Get it out of my sight!" My three sons have never gotten over that. Each one wanted it!

Mike always felt responsible and protective of the folks. Of course they were very independent people and didn't require much attention until their later years. In the last ten years Mom lived in Newberg in an apartment that Mike had built onto his house. It was not uncommon for him to come in early with a rosebud he had found in the garden or a dish of fresh raspberries he had just picked. There was a strong bond between Mike and Mom. He visited Dad regularly at Friendsview. Of course, Dad became a bit forgetful and complained that he was neglected, but in reality this was not the case.

Dad was always an individualist. My husband could view him objectively and saw lots of humor in Dad's makeup. He gave every bride a rolling pin. He always wore a bright red hunting hat to weddings. Mom would not be seen with Dad's outfits so they arrived separately. Dad always ridiculed Mom for her "high falutin" ideas and friends. However, they survived all this a good long time. They celebrated their seventieth anniversary on July 29, 1978. Mom died at ninety years of age and Dad at ninety-nine.

*D*AD ALWAYS had two weeks vacation from his job as a letter carrier. I remember a month at Newport when the folks had rented a cottage at Nye Beach. It was a big undertaking to get there as we first took the Southern Pacific train from Salem to Albany, then transferred to another train on which we rode to Toledo. Mom took along an ample lunch for us to eat enroute. At Toledo we boarded the ferry and crossed Yaquina Bay, then a horse-drawn dray hauled us up the hill and finally deposited us at our cottage. It was a full day's trip and very exciting. Dad came over later and joined the family.

Another time Dad hired a man with a pickup truck to haul us to a pasture area west of Falls City. We were deposited at a spot near a brook with groceries, a cook stove, tent, bedding, clothing, et cetera. It was on this vacation that Dad found a collie puppy for us which we named Goldie. She was a beautiful dog with a shag nose and a white ruff around her neck. No one ever came to check on us or collect payment for squatting in the field. After two weeks the truck driver came for us and we rode back to Salem.

When Mike was about ten we joined with another family with two children slightly younger than us, and their Dad drove us to Neskowin and left us there. Of course, there were two tents this time for the seven people. The folks chose a nice, grassy spot in a pasture and turned in for the night after Mom had cooked a succulent meal. Goldie awakened us all with her incessant barking and it turned out that we had camped in the path of a herd of cows and a bull. Subsequent events were quite exciting as Mom tried to shinny up a dew-drenched poplar and slid back almost as much as she advanced. Dad armed himself with an axe and Mike with the rolling pin. Needless to say, much of the next day was spent moving the tents to a different campsite. Mom never lived this down and it proved a delightful tale back at the home church with many embellishments.

We lived in town, but always kept one cow and sold milk to various neighbors. Mike and I delivered this milk, probably three times a week. For this Mom gave us each fifty cents a month, which we thought was tremendous. Dad bought the family's first car when Mike was sixteen and he sold Beauty (the cow) before the car was delivered. I was the only one in the family who could drive, and I was too young for a license. (A widower in the church had started to teach me on his farm when I was ten.) We had some hair-raising experiences as Dad tried to drive. He would get to an intersection, holler "Gee," and make a sharp right. We would all be catapulted to the side of the car. Dad never used an intersection with a traffic light if he could avoid it. He said it wasted gas and necessitated changing gears. Why do that?

During World War I, Dad couldn't resist the opportunity to sell his Studebaker for more than he had paid. Thus, of course, he had trouble replacing the car. He thought it quite unnecessary to use a car—except for trips or to care for his sheep—so he bought an old Chevy of questionable vintage. Mom did not like this car and Dad eventually traded it in for a pickup truck. Mom told him she would not ride in a truck, and in fact, the step was so high she couldn't have done so. This did not deter Dad a particle. He bought the truck and shared it with his sheep. Mom got places in any way she could.

*U*PON GRADUATION in 1928, Milo enrolled at the Portland Bible Institute where he received a diploma in 1931. He then enrolled at Willamette University, receiving his Bachelor of Arts degree in 1934 with a major in Spanish. One of the interesting papers he wrote at Portland Bible Institute had to do with Milo's call to the ministry. It gives a glimpse of Milo's writing skill in this significant period of his schooling. He was probably thinking carefully about his own future as he developed this paper about the role of a pastor in the local church. It is entitled, "The Pastor as an Executive," and it was written on January 20, 1931. His teacher gave him an A grade for this particular writing assignment. (Text available at www.barclaypress.com/Ross.)

Our maternal great-grandmother was a painter in oils, and it was thought that Mike inherited her talent. He showed ability early on, and a correspondence course was financed for him. He wanted to study violin, but Dad would not permit this. "No son of mine is going to fiddle at a dance." So he compromised by providing the art course. This probably helped Mike obtain the job at the sign shop. Later on he took art courses at the University of Oregon summer school in Portland. His professors there were very encouraging. They felt that his work was salable. There was a collage of the creation that was particularly impressive. As far as I know, I have the only remaining example of his work, which is a still life in pastels. Mike was often impetuous in his movements and broke his wrists at least two times. He was definitely left-handed, and the fractures seriously affected his art work, which he finally abandoned.

One summer Mike and I went to University of Oregon summer school classes in Portland. (It must have been the same summer he married.) He was pastoring at Rosedale Friends Church at the time, and offerings were small. Thelma (his coupe) refused to run without gas, and one Sunday night the inevitable occurred as we drove along Macadam Road in southwest Portland. Mike eased Thelma over onto the dock, took off his shoes, and went to sleep. I was awakened about 5 a.m. with a flashlight shining in the window, and a voice behind a badge asked gruffly what we were doing. I said we had run out of gas, but he did not seem convinced. He asked for the car's title. I couldn't find it in the glove compartment and tried to awaken Mike to look for it. Mike was dead asleep, and the cop was certain he was intoxicated. What an adventure it was to finally get him aroused. Well, the cop then went off to get gas for us at an all-night station, and returned in time for us to drive to our rooms on the eastside before classes. Mike was very peeved about this and said he wouldn't have had to drive the extra mileage if the cop hadn't brought the gas. He could have gone directly to school. "In your rumpled clothes?" Of course! Nothing proud about Mike!

MIKE STARTED going to Twin Rocks early in his teens. I don't remember anything unusual about Mike at Twin Rocks, but his future sister-in-law, Florence Ritter Lehman, says she remembers him for his unusual humor. As a sibling, I was not impressed by that. He probably met his wife, Helen Ritter, at the camp and their courtship continued when he went to Portland Bible Institute since the Ritter girls lived close by and attended Piedmont Friends Church.

Mike and Helen were married at Sunnyside Friends Church (now Reedwood) on September 12, 1934. They then were pastors at Rosedale Friends Church.

We have searched for wedding pictures, but there must not have been any. Mike had been pastoring at least a year at Rosedale before his marriage. He must have been going to Willamette University during this time. A boyfriend and I spent considerable time decorating the parsonage in what we considered the right touches. We equipped the privy with cobs, a Sears catalog, et cetera, and the parsonage itself had toilet tissue just everywhere and rice in the bed. We waited and waited for some reaction to our efforts, but it was several months before we learned that two of the parishioners had come over to check the parsonage and had thought the decorations were quite indecent and improper for their pastor, so they had cleaned everything out.

*H*ELEN NEVER fully recovered her health after her third preg-
nancy. She suffered from hypertension plus kidney problems
during their Seattle pastorate. One of the most selfless actions I have
known were the trips made by two parishioners to the parsonage to
help Helen during this difficult time. This was done by one of the
Woodward families.

I don't really know if Mike felt his work in Seattle was complete, if he needed to move because the boys were ready for college,
or if he felt he must get out of the pastorate for Helen's sake. At any
rate, he moved the family to Salem, built a home with Dad's help in
the Keizer area, and took a position at George Fox College.

On their last trip to Vancouver, B.C., we bought a dress for
Helen to wear to the inaugural of Mike's presidency at George Fox.
She was too weak to stand, but the sales clerk was most gracious in
staying late to fit Helen. She wore the dress for her burial.

The Ross Descendants

Milo Clifton Ross was born January 17, 1911, in Salem, Oregon, to Clifton Ross and Carrie Bernice Prince Ross. Milo married Helen Ritter of Portland, Oregon. Their three children are: **Stephen Bradford Ross** born in 1935, **Larry Duncan Ross** born in 1937, and **Nancy Carolyn Ross Brown** born in 1943.

STEPHEN married Mary Louise Hatcher and they had three children: **Kimberlee** Laine Ross, **Kirk** Bradford Ross, and **Kelly** Bruce Ross.

Kimberlee married William Timothy Robbins. Their seven children are: Brandy Robbins Geary, Amy Corinne Robbins Bell Noyce, Derek Robbins, Brian Robbins, Darci Robbins, Timmy Robbins, and Traci Robbins Mammen. Brandy married Tim Geary and they have two children: Kendall Laine Geary and Brandon Geary. Brian married Kristen and they have three children: Nathan Robbins, Daniel Robbins, and Caroline Robbins. Amy married Michael Bell and they have two children: Madison Bell and Shane Bell.

Kirk married Thuy "Lauren" Tran and they have two children: Tessa Tran Ross and Adam Ross.

LARRY married Shirley Annette Cadd Ross and they had three children: **Debra** Lorraine Ross Lee-Martell, **Laurie** Ann Ross, and **Shelly** Lynn Ross Carson.

Debra married Michael Norman Lee and they had one son Tyler Ross Lee. After their divorce Debra married Allan Lee-Martell.

Laurie married Mark James Beecroft and had two children: Chad Alvin Beecroft and Alexandra Danielle Beecroft Milburn. Chad married Alia Ruth Paquette and they have two children: Jones Mark Beecroft and Eames Denson Beecroft. Alexandra married Brian Milbourn and they have a daughter Cadence Jane Milbourn. After her divorce Laurie married Daniel Alan Van Dyke and they had two children: Jace Alan Van Dyke and Cameron Ross Van Dyke. Jace married Samantha Jayne Rials and have a son Finnigan August Van Dyke.

Shelly married Tony Carson, and they later divorced with no children.

NANCY married David Carey Brown and they have two children: **Jonathan** Michael Brown and **Daniel** Volle Brown.

Jonathan had Amber Kathleen Brown with Tammy Gibson. He married Christy Ann Egli Papulski who had two daughters: Morgan Ann Papulski and Alyx Jillee Papulski.

Daniel married Laura Ann Snyder and they have three children: Elijah Ross Brown and Jesse Raymond Brown, and Lydia Faith Brown.

Milo's wife, Helen, died in 1954 after years of poor health. A year later he married **Alice Hope Gaddis Wheeler** who had two children: **Elletta Ann Wheeler Eichenberger Kennison** born in 1933 and **Ned G Wheeler** born in 1939. Milo and Alice made a successful effort in bonding the two families together so no one thinks of step family.

ELLETA married Theodore Wayne Eichenberger and they had four children: **Ronda** Lynn Eichenberger Hutchison Greenawalt, **Randal** Wayne Eichenberger, **Dennis** Wade Eichenberger, and **Karen** Ann Eichenberger Hust Lollis.

Ronda married Steven Alan Hutchison and they had two children: Kyle Dwayne Hutchison and Lisa Marie Hutchison Rios. Kyle married Jennifer Tan and they have one son Owen Tan Hutchison. Lisa married Raul Valdez Rios and they have three children: Lucia Bella Rios, Emilia Cristina Rios, and Joaquin Steven Rios. After their divorce Ronda married Phillip Schuyler Greenawalt.

Randy married Kari Anderson and they had two children: Michael Wayne Eichenberger and Michelle Kathleen Eichenberger. Michael married Sara Anderson and they had one daughter Dakota Rayne Eichenberger.

Dennis married Charmaine Brighton who had two children: Cassandra Brighton and Heaven Brighton. Cassandra married Ernest Castillo and they have two children: Arianna Isabella Castillo and Roman Enrique Castillo.

Karen married William Pepper Hust and they had one son Ryan Samuel Hust. After their divorce she married Kevin Michael Lollis who had one son Connor Jan Lollis.

NED married Geneva Gaye Nordyke and had two children: **Wade** Robert Wheeler and **Cheryl** Lynn Wheeler dos Remedios.

Wade married Stephanie Grace Bertholf and they have two girls: Siri Elisabeth Wheeler and Anika Maria Wheeler.

Cheryl married Ricardo dos Remedios and they have a daughter Angelina Marie dos Remedios.

After his divorce, Ned married Camilla Maria Lust Claeys and they had two children: **Jacob** Albert Wheeler and **Miriam** Alicia Wheeler. Jacob married Rachel Alta Liles and they have a daughter Amelia Joy Wheeler.

Index

CPSIA information can be obtained at www.ICGtesting.com
Printed in the USA
LVOW04s1223190815

450578LV00011B/141/P